HARRY BRUCE
True Tales of Industrial Leadership

HARRY BRUCE
True Tales of Industrial Leadership

F.K. Plous

HARRY BRUCE
True Tales of Industrial Leadership

Designed and published by Luna Creative
Knoxville, Tennessee 37922
lunacreates.com

Trade paperback ISBN: 978-1-7358056-3-4

For my wife Vivienne and my mentors and colleagues,
Douglas S. Warner, Robert Stucker, Alfred E. Perlman,
James W. Bennett, Joseph L. Frye, Jr., Gayton Germane, Fred W. Frailey,
Robert Schwarz, Leon Reed, William Piper, Newton Morton,
C. Warren Neel, Mark Gocke MD, Richard Senior, and Clifford Harris

–HARRY BRUCE

TABLE OF CONTENTS

AUTHOR'S PREFACE

I first met Harry Bruce sometime in the late 1970s, when he was
the senior vice-president of marketing at the Illinois Central Gulf
Railroad in Chicago. Something I had contributed to one of the
local newspapers had caught his attention, suggesting to him that
I had some sort of railroad background. He asked me to come in
and assist the ICG with some writing assignments, from executive speeches and sales brochures to articles for the railroad trade
media. The money was good, the company congenial, and the
inside views of the railroad industry were pure gold to a writer who
had started as a brakeman at 18 and was now hanging out at the
corporate level of a Class 1 carrier.

When the railroad's CEO died suddenly in 1983 and Bruce was
named as his successor, my assignment changed in ways that my
railroad background had not prepared me for. As chief executive
officer, Bruce was deeply concerned about two issues which many
CEOs are unprepared for: corporate governance—the legal obligations of corporate managers to the shareholders who own the

company—and leadership—the behaviors, attitudes, beliefs, motivations, and sense of obligation that enable certain individuals to inspire others to believe them and follow them into challenging new endeavors.

Bruce was genuinely intrigued by leadership because he had come into it accidentally. As an indifferent high-school student and a college drop-out, he had never heard or thought about leadership until a test he took as a U.S. Army draftee showed that he had "leadership potential" and he was sent to Officer Candidate School. The test proved to be right, but Bruce never lost his fascination with its ability to divine his potential. How did the Army know he was leadership material? What, exactly, made somebody a leader?

Bruce didn't get much of a handle on the subject until 1972, when he went to work for the Western Pacific Railroad and encountered its new CEO, the legendary American railroad-rescuer Alfred E. Perlman. Even after working for Perlman and winning Perlman's praise for his leader-ship skills, Bruce remained puzzled about the nature of leadership itself.

Bruce sent me on a deep dive into leadership literature in order to get to the bottom of the subject, but we never found a real consensus among the many authors we read. Instead, Bruce examined the leaders he had encountered in his own background and discovered behaviors that the popular leadership authors had largely overlooked.

In "leadership without portfolio" he found daring personalities who undertook initiatives for which they had no formal authority for from their superiors. From a beloved mentor, the late Stanford University Professor Gayton Germane, he learned the "hidden value of the unsolved problem". Leaders often emerge by tackling and solving the problems that their predecessors had given up on.

As Bruce contributed articles on these subjects to a growing list of professional publications and textbooks, his stature grew, and not only in the railroad industry, but in his second love, academia. After retiring in 1989, he resumed lecturing and writing on corporate governance and leadership. His students, particularly those at his alma mater, the Transportation Economics Department at the University of Tennessee's College of Business Administration, have now gone on to professional careers. Harry Bruce's books and magazine articles continue to be in high demand with each successive generation of students.

This book is an attempt to show how a college dropout went on to become a leader and a teacher of leadership to subsequent generations. It would take another book to explain what an honor it's been to write it.

F.K. Plous
Chicago
December 2023

CHAPTER 1

IT WAS ABOUT THE TRAINS

When Harry J. Bruce arrived in Knoxville in 1956 seeking a
Master's Degree from the Transportation Economics Department
of University of Tennessee's School of Business Administration,
he had arrived by an unusual route.

The 25-year-old from Short Hills, New Jersey was an Army veteran
who had been pulled from the ranks and sent to Officer Candidate
School. Newly married, Bruce had been lurching through a series
of unusual educational and workplace experiences for the last
five years.

Bruce had little inclination—and even less motivation—to pursue a
career when he graduated from high school in 1949. Although his
high-school performance was, in his words, "undistinguished," his
family had nursed higher hopes. They hoped he would follow in
his father's footsteps, a research chemist, whose first job had been

at Thomas Edison's laboratory in West Orange, N.J. Bruce's older brother, Jack, also went into chemistry.

Sensing that young Harry needed a little direction to find a career track—and also to keep him out of trouble—the family dispatched him to Bethany College in Lindsborg, Kansas, 20 miles south of Salina.

It was not the answer that Bruce or his parents were looking for.

"I believe I must have set the all-time Bethany College record for non-study," Bruce recalled.

His problem was not laziness but focus. Bruce was full of energy, but instead of hitting the books, he found a part-time job as a night-shift baggage handler at the local railroad station. From time to time, he worked as a gandy dancer, swinging a spike maul and leaning into a 6-foot crowbar while re-aligning the Missouri Pacific's tracks. At one point, he worked as a roughneck in the local oil fields. Scholastic activity didn't seem to be his forte, and it was showing. After three years of schooling, he dropped out and slunk back to New Jersey.

Neither Bruce nor his family could put their finger on the problem at the time, but, in retrospect, it's clear that Bruce was seeking work with mystique. It's not a word commonly used by career counselors or college advisors, nor does Bruce use it, but such people are unconsciously driven to seek an element of mystery in their work because, without it, the work—and the education and preparation leading to it—are simply not exciting enough to keep the subject motivated and focused.

It was about the trains

For Bruce that mystique was found in only one kind of work:
railroading.

It started, he said, when he was very little. In the days before air
conditioning, summer heat and humidity drove every family that
could afford it out of the smoky industrial cities of the Northeast
to the mountains or the shore.

For the Bruce family, escape meant traveling south sixty miles to
the little New Jersey seashore community of Manasquan, where
they rented quarters in a big frame rooming house just blocks
from the ocean. Little Harry loved it, but what he loved most

wasn't fishing from the pier or watching the boats go through the drawbridge. Instead, he hung around the railroad depot and watched Mr. Purdy hand-crank the crossing gates down as the train approached. Best of all, it meant positioning himself on the platform exactly opposite from the spot where the steam locomotive stopped. The squeal of the air brakes, the hissing of steam, and the hot sparks and cinders falling from the rumbling firebox held him in a grip that he still talks about more than 80 years later.

The mystique of the machinery did not exert its full effect without the human element—the engineer who commanded the great machine and the fireman who kept its boiler content with precisely the right amount of water and coal to maintain the ideal steam pressure. To little Harry, these were the kinds of characters children seek in stories—superhuman beings with awesome powers derived from following complex rituals that were opaque to mere humans.

When 21-year-old Harry returned from Kansas in the spring of 1952 without a college degree, he finally had found his passion.

"I announced to my parents that I had hired out as a fireman on the Delaware, Lackawanna & Western Railroad in Hoboken," he wrote in his privately published 2003 memoirs. "You can imagine the row that set off."

Bruce was ecstatic. He was working for the local railroad, where he found even the dreariest labor to be exciting and meaningful. For a week before he actually climbed into a locomotive cab, Bruce apprenticed by cleaning the ash pit where the steam locomotives dumped the sulfurous "clinkers" from their spent fires. He loved it.

"My boss worked me hard, but he taught me lessons as well: how to lift and swing a shovel without wearing myself out, how to get along with fellow employees, how to show proper deference to superiors," Bruce later wrote. "He also helped me to get oriented by explaining what went on in the engine terminal. I came to understand why certain things had to be done a certain way and at a certain time. Even a dedicated rail fan may find cleaning out an ash pit a little lacking in glamor, but to me it was the most exciting thing I had ever done. I literally could not wait to get to work each day."

CHAPTER 2

THE FIRST OF MANY MENTORS

That foreman turned out to be a critical figure in the young man's development. While Bruce had encountered many teachers in his fitful progress through grade school and his aborted attempt at college, the boss at the roundhouse turned out to be the first one worthy of the title mentor. The encounter with the roundhouse foreman proved so decisive that it seems to have programmed Bruce to seek out and even to unconsciously attract mentors. In the future, wherever he went, and particularly when he faced a career decision, an experienced older man always seemed to turn up with exactly the guidance Bruce needed. These mentors seemed to sense that Bruce not only needed their advice, but that he would heed it as well.

After a week in the ash pit, Bruce was assigned to his first trip as a student fireman on a freight locomotive. When he climbed into the cab and got his first glimpse of the stern, white-haired engineer checking him out through wire-rimmed spectacles, he felt himself to be looking at "the forbidden face of God." When the engineer finished giving young Bruce the once-over, the student felt that he was hearing the voice of God as well.

"Sit down, boy—there, on the fireman's box—and mind you don't make any mess in my cab!"

Encounters with mentors are not always warm and welcoming but Bruce always listened and learned.

Lessons, lessons, lessons—at last a true education
The sting of a rebuff never stung for long, because each rebuff contained something Bruce found precious—a lesson. At college, lessons came in books and lectures. On the Lackawanna, they came from the intimate interaction between men and machines

and the chatter between the crew members. Bruce voraciously digested every correction and instruction about train and locomotive operations. He learned how to keep steam up in the boiler and to administering precisely distributed doses of coal to the firebox. He learned how to call out the wayside block signals to the engineer as the train made its way down the main line. Bruce had to keep looking backwards out of the cab window during switching operations so he could relay hand signals from the conductor and brakeman to the engineer as the crew "on the ground" coupled and uncoupled freight cars for spotting on factory sidings. There were few idle moments, and every one of the busy ones was filled with lessons.

The railroad made Bruce what he had never been before—a student—and what he learned about studying, learning, and seeking out mentors stayed with him.

Those lessons followed him to his next adventure.

CHAPTER 3

"GREETINGS"

"After six months on the job, I came home to find a letter inform-
ing me that my local draft board had found its own solution to my
career problems," he said.

After completing basic training at the Army's tank-driving
school at Fort Knox in Kentucky, Bruce assumed he was headed
to Korea, where the bloody "UN police action" was raging along
the 38th parallel.

Bruce never shipped out. His Army aptitude and psychological
tests indicated that he had leadership potential. Instead of sending him to the battlefield, the Army sent him to Officer Candidate
School at Fort Benning, Georgia.

Talking the talk and walking the walk at the "Murder Board"
As part of his command training, Bruce received instruction in a
skill that most outsiders rarely associate with the Army—public

speaking. He turned out to be good at it, especially the variety of public speaking known in the Army as "Murder Board," where an officer candidate lectures a panel of senior officers and noncoms on a complex battlefield or logistical problem and then undergoes a withering barrage of questions designed to catch the speaker unprepared, uninformed, or just too nervous to handle the incoming fire.

Bruce turned out to be a survivor—cool, unflappable, courteous, articulate—and made a point to be properly informed and back-grounded. It was an accomplishment that turned out to be unexpectedly valuable in every phase of his future career. Although it was not known at the time, behavioral scientists have since established that as many as 77 percent of Americans fear public speaking and that 30 to 40 percent are not just reluctant to get up and address a room full of people, but are actually terrified of doing so.

That fear creates a little-understood dynamic—when people who are afraid to speak in public are addressed by a speaker who appears confident, relaxed, and in command of himself, they experience the speaker as powerful. They accept the speaker's ideas and confer on him or her that precious attribute known as leadership.

Harry Bruce felt something of that dynamic when he addressed the panel. When he finished his officer training and was posted to Germany as a second lieutenant, it continued to fascinate him. The Army seemed to think he had something called "leadership potential," but what exactly was it? Who had it and who didn't? How could you tell?

Cupid + math = college

Bruce might have pursued that question further as a rising Army officer, but love intervened. While on assignment in Germany, he met Vivienne Jennings, a young art-school graduate from Alton, Illinois, who had been hired by the Army to guide their personnel through Europe's great museums, palaces, and cathedrals. Marriage plans were soon made, and, when Bruce's hitch was up, he moved back to New Jersey and spent the interval leading up to the wedding in the setting where he felt most comfortable—as a fireman on the Lackawanna Railroad—but this time was different.

Buoyed by his successful Army training and an educational breakthrough, Bruce now turned his sights on completing his truncated college education. Rutgers University was nearby, and the GI Bill could cover the tuition. Bruce's brother introduced him to a neighbor who was the provost at Rutgers. On reviewing his grades from Bethany, however, the provost noted a serious weakness in Bruce's mathematical background. He wouldn't be able to get into Rutgers until he showed sufficient skill in math.

Not to worry.

"We have an excellent practical course at our Newark campus that could help you," the provost said. "First- and second-year algebra, plus geometry and trigonometry. You fix that up and then we can take a look at you."

Bruce did "fix that up" by attending night classes until 10 p.m. and then heading to the Lackawanna yards in Hoboken to spend the rest of the night working as a fireman on a diesel switch engine. His work-study program did its job, yielding all As and Bs, but once he had alleviated himself of his math deficit, it wasn't Rutgers that "took a look at him". It was Kent State in Ohio. A kind professor at Rutgers told him that the business school at Kent State offered something Rutgers didn't—a degree in industrial engineering with a specialty in transportation.

Pausing barely long enough to marry his fiancee, Bruce entered the Kent State program and emerged 18 months later with a precious degree that offered him entry to the managerial ranks of the transportation industry. If he wanted to join a railroad and rise to an executive position, this was his chance.

Once again, a benign mentor appeared, beckoning him toward further study and greater ambitions. This was coming to be a theme in Bruce's career—whenever he found himself pausing at the crossroads to make a decision, a kindly academic took an interest in him and helped him clarify his prospects. This time, it was Newton Morton, a former Pennsylvania Railroad executive who had joined the faculty at Kent State and helped Bruce take the next step. Morton advised Bruce to continue his studies at the graduate level at either Michigan State or the Transportation Economics Department in the University of Tennessee's College of Business Administration.

Bruce evaluated the two schools, chose UT, and he and his now pregnant wife loaded their gear into their 1953 Buick and headed for Knoxville.

CHAPTER 4

UT: LAUNCH PAD TO A CAREER

The UT Transportation Economics Department had some of
the most respected faculty in the nation. Its professors shuttled
between academia and business, sharing practical lessons with
the students that they might otherwise not have learned until
they joined the transportation industry. Bruce seemed caught
between the academic and commercial poles of transportation.
Should he aim at studying logistics and teach it, or should he
plan to enter the industry and practice it? Both choices seemed
equally attractive.

UT also gave Bruce an opportunity to stretch the lecture muscles
he developed in the Army. Although he did not receive a teaching assistantship, he filled in for the legendary Professor Joe Frye
when the latter became ill. Frye's students genuinely enjoyed
the clear, measured speaking style that Bruce had developed as
a young Army officer. They got a particular kick out of something none of their other instructors provided—true tales from a

locomotive cab. Bruce's training in public speaking had merged
with his railroad experience and produced a lecturer the students
couldn't wait to hear.

Once Professor Frye recovered, he thanked Bruce in a highly
original way—he called a reporter friend at the *Knoxville Journal*
and told him that one of his students with a talent for economic
geography had made a study revealing that Tennessee no longer
was in the "colonial stage" of economic development—supplying
other states with raw materials while importing finished goods.
Instead, Tennessee now had a "mature" economy that was producing a wide variety of industrial and consumer products for out-of-
state customers. The story, which quoted Bruce, was published
April 3, 1959. It was not the last time Bruce's work would appear
in print.

More mentors appear
Perhaps the greatest gift UT gave Bruce was the chance to network
with experts outside the university—including leading professors
of transportation at other universities. D. Phillip Locklin at the
University of Illinois asked Bruce to pursue a doctorate from that
institution, and Bruce strongly considered it.

Professors weren't the only stars in the Transportation Economics
Department's firmament. There were luminaries from the transportation industry itself, successful executives who were willing
to share practical insider experience not normally available to
those still in school. Bruce listened to all of them and wavered
before making his next move. Would it be more academia, where
he now had considerable experience, or the executive suite, where
he had none?

Curiously, it was an academic who urged Bruce toward industry. Professor James Bennett, who headed UT's Transportation Economics Department, had a hunch that Bruce would do well in business and suggested that he meet with a friend of his, a recruiter from the United States Steel Corp. named D. Harry Headly, who was in Knoxville at the time looking for promising new hires. Headly immediately offered Bruce a job with U.S. Steel at its Pittsburgh headquarters. Bruce hesitated at first, as he already had been offered the chance to study for a doctorate at the University of Illinois, but Bennett gently nudged him toward the job offer.

"He said to me, 'Mr. Bruce, U.S. Steel has made you an offer. You will not go to the University of Illinois.' He saw that academia was not for me. He knew I was better suited to industry, but with some teaching on the side."

Bruce, still torn between business and academia, completed his master's degree and took the job offer.

"Quite frankly, it was the money," he said. "Vivienne was pregnant with our second child and U.S. Steel was offering $700 a month. That looked to me like all the money in the world in 1959."

Not your usual start up the executive ladder
Once settled in Pittsburgh, Bruce took a deep dive into the world of U.S. Steel, spending his days in the 8-week training course the giant company administered to all executive recruits. True to his style, he consumed all the course material and quickly digested it with an air of confidence appropriate for a fast-rising young executive. Inwardly, however, Bruce was far from confident about his future and was full of troubling doubts.

"Even with my new master's degree, I couldn't help but wonder: How was I supposed to contribute anything to a company that dominated its industry?" Bruce later wrote, "U.S. Steel seemingly was a company that already had all the answers. They were the world leader in steelmaking. How could I possibly provide them with anything they didn't already have?"

Further complicating Bruce's baptism at U.S. Steel was the not-always-good-natured hazing he had to put up with from some of his fellow executive recruits.

"Most of them came from the Ivy League schools or from the better-known state universities in the East," Bruce said. "When they found out I was a graduate of the University of Tennessee they gave me lots of ribbing—was it hard getting used to wearing shoes to work and had I shot any 'b'ar' in the Smokies?" Bruce said it felt strange to be taunted by easterners for his presumed Tennessee associations. He'd only spent two years of his life there, and his accent, then as now, was pure North Jersey.

"What do we do now?"
Bruce's self doubts were further amplified by the situation that greeted him when he joined U.S. Steel's transportation depart-ment—the company's employees were on strike—the longest strike in the history of the American steel industry. No products were being shipped and no raw materials were coming in. The com-pany's transportation department had nothing to do.

A break quickly came when Bruce's superior, vice president of Transportation Dr. E. Grosvenor Plowman, learned about Bruce's

skills at research, writing, and speaking. Plowman, along with his heir-apparent Kenneth L. Vore, did lots of public speaking, and the hiatus generated by the steel strike gave them even more time to address industry and customer groups around the country. They needed scripts and research, and Bruce, with his Army speaker training and his fresh academic laurels, supplied both at a rate that matched their busy speaking schedules.

Bruce caught a second break several months later when another newcomer turned up in the U.S. Steel transportation department. Dr. Gayton E. Germane, a Stanford University professor of business, was on a three-year sabbatical with a double agenda—to find real-world examples of industrial transportation practices to bring back to his students while refreshing a major industry with the latest insights from academia.

The professor's new recruit

Germane immediately enlisted Bruce in his first effort, a complete review of the department's records—all paper in those days—for any evidence of problems the staff had been unable to solve.

They found one. Mouldering in U.S. Steel's files was an unfinished inquiry into whether some of the transportation tasks inside a steel mill could be automated. The first computers were coming into industrial use and U.S. Steel wanted to know whether the right software could direct unmanned, radio-controlled railcars to deliver iron ore, coke, and limestone to the blast furnace while other dummy railcars carried fresh pig iron to the sites where it would be processed into steel and steel products.

The study Bruce reviewed had never generated any follow-up. Its plodding language, which lacked both vigor and focus, never reached a conclusion or suggested any next steps. A test vehicle had never been built, and the report provided no timetable or milestones to lead to a launch.

Bruce resolved to re-open the effort and bring it to a successful conclusion.

CHAPTER 5

THE SECRET BLESSING OF THE UNSOLVED PROBLEM

"Germane taught me a valuable lesson," Bruce said: "An employee who solves a problem which others have given up on gets two or three times more credit from his superiors than one who simply solves a problem that's never been tackled before. I wanted to revive that automation study."

The problem, Bruce quickly realized, was the report's weak presentation. Its language was rambling and inconclusive. A young Army officer presenting it to his superiors would have been cut to ribbons by the review panel because the poorly organized material offered no basis for making a decision.

Bruce replaced the turgid corporate prose with the shorter, more conversational language he had used in his military presentations, but it was his artist wife who came up with the solution that really caught the eyes of Bruce's superiors.

"Vivienne said, 'This reads like a boring corporate report—you need to make it more like a comic book,'" Bruce recalled. Mrs. Bruce proceeded to do just that.

"I sketched ideas out on the back of an envelope and my wife took it from there," he said. "As soon as the kids were in bed, Vivienne would set up her easel and start drawing. Vivienne was a highly gifted charcoal-sketch artist. She had an amazing ability to convert verbal information into expressive, appealing pictures that anyone could understand. Instead of the typical late-fifties corporate report, we turned in an illustrated survey of the problem and its likely solutions, with the text and illustrations closely coordinated to make abstract ideas seem real and exciting."

The "comic book" worked. Germane loved it. So did Plowman and Vore, who passed it on to U.S. Steel's partners in the venture.

"The Westinghouse and Union Switch & Signal people were even more enthusiastic than the ones at U.S. Steel," Bruce said. The three corporations issued a magazine-sized booklet titled, "The Future of Automated Movement in the Iron and Steel Industry," using Bruce's language and his wife's black and white charcoal illustrations. The project regained its momentum, an automated test vehicle named "Spook" was built, and the three sponsors presented the Bruces with a certificate of commendation.

"It was at U.S. Steel that my career first took off," Bruce said. "Vivienne was the booster rocket that lofted my career into space."

U.S. Steel begins to study transportation and builds a new market
His climb was rapid. Bruce now was detailed to U.S. Steel's laboratory in Monroeville, Pennsylvania. Historically, Monroeville's research had focused solely on problems of steel production. Thanks to the Bruces' breakthrough document, the labs now began to research transportation. His original approach to transportation problems soon paid off again with a technological breakthrough that enabled U.S. Steel to enter into a new market by selling one of its waste products.

How do we get rid of this stuff?
The product was pitch, a heavy, dirty by-product of the coke-making process made up almost entirely of carbon. Pitch was highly valued by the aluminum industry because carbon is

essential in making the electrodes that generate the heat needed to smelt aluminum out of bauxite ore. U.S. Steel was unable to sell its pitch to the aluminum industry because the smelters insisted the pitch be delivered in liquid form in tank cars.

Most of the big aluminum smelters were in Canada, and, on the 1,000-mile trip from the mills in Gary, Indiana, to Chicoutimi, Quebec, the pitch solidified in the tank cars and could not be unloaded until the entire car was reheated. In the dead of winter, it could take two weeks to re-liquify an entire load, an expensive process that tied up employees and rail equipment that were needed for other tasks.

Here again, Bruce, still early in his career, demonstrated one of those qualities that most experts agree is a prime element in leadership—an eagerness to take on tasks that other managers have avoided.

"What if somebody built a tank car with an interior heating system that could keep the pitch liquified through the entire trip?" Bruce wondered. "The car could be emptied immediately upon arrival and returned to the railroad for another load."

Bruce turned to the Vapor Corporation of Evanston, Illinois, a longtime supplier of steam-heating systems for railroad passenger cars. The Vapor engineers designed a system of coils capable of circulating a liquid heating medium through the interior of a tank car full of pitch. To heat the circulating liquid, the engineers mounted a propane-fired heater and a tank of propane on the tank car's running board. To make sure that the system worked, Bruce accompanied the first shipment on its week-long journey from the U.S. Steel mill in Gary to Chicoutimi, Quebec, riding in the caboose along with a bank of monitoring equipment directly behind the experimental tank car at the rear of the train.

The Thermo-Temp tank car worked. The cargo of pitch stayed liquid and was emptied immediately upon its arrival at the Canadian smelter. A promotional campaign followed, and U.S. Steel began selling and shipping its pitch in increasing volumes.

Privately, however, Bruce had qualms about the new technology he had developed. During the trip to Canada, the experimental tank car developed an overheated wheel bearing—a "hot box"— that was fortunately detected by the crew of a freight train passing on the opposite track. Their hand signals from the caboose alerted the crew of Bruce's train to stop and set the smoking tank car out on a siding, where Bruce and car repairman quenched the hot bearing and replaced the wheel truck so the car could proceed on a following train.

"If that bearing had burst into flame and ignited the propane in the heater, my car and I could have been blown to Kingdom Come," Bruce said. "I realized I had designed a rolling bomb."

Luckily, no other cars ever developed the same problem. U.S. Steel's pitch business continued to grow, eventually winning sales of $30 million per year, a very substantial sum in the early 1960s and a major coup for the young executive whose initiative had made the new business possible. Several years later, the heated tank cars were replaced by insulated cars that kept the pitch liquid without a supplementary heating source.

CHAPTER 6

LEARNING WHILE TEACHING

Bruce's heated-tank-car initiative had made him a young star at U.S. Steel and the corporation's go-to guy on temperature problems in freight shipping. He also remained something of a fixture in academia, lecturing once a week in the business school at the University of Pittsburgh and two nights a week at Duquesne University. He kept his writing up as well, steadily contributing articles on industrial shipping problems and economic geography to a variety of transportation journals.

Thawing out U.S. Steel's frozen thinking

He kept finding transportation problems at U.S. Steel, including one of the company's oldest and most persistent—iron ore frozen so hard it could not be unloaded from railroad hopper cars. During the winter, when the Great Lakes were frozen and ore boats could not deliver their cargo to the mills, U.S. Steel switched its iron-ore sourcing from the Minnesota Iron Range to Venezuela. The South

American ore was shipped in giant ocean-going bulk freighters to Philadelphia, where it was trans-loaded, still smoking-warm, into hopper cars for shipment to the ore-storage yard at Pittsburgh.

There was a problem though. When crossing the Alleghenies, the ore froze so solid it could not be tipped out of the cars on a rotary dumper at Pittsburgh. Employees wasted hours banging on the car sides with sledge hammers and inserting steam lances into the contents before the ore loosened. Curiously, neither U.S. Steel nor the Pennsylvania Railroad, whose 4-tracked main line connected Philadelphia and Pittsburgh, had ever made any effort to understand how the freezing occurred. The problem dated back at least to the founding of U.S. Steel in 1901 and nobody seemed to know or care what to do about it.

First get the numbers

Bruce, now driven by scientific curiosity and a lust for more career success, sent a couple of loaded ore cars to Philadelphia, where the Budd Company owned a cryogenic chamber it used to test the heat-holding properties of its stainless-steel passenger cars. The Budd engineers subjected the ore cars to a controlled freeze and quickly answered Bruce's questions—the ore was not losing heat from the open tops of the cars as had been expected. The top two or three inches of the ore froze, forming a barrier that prevented the underlying lading from shedding more heat into the slipstream, but the steel sides of the cars were acting like radiators, rapidly conducting heat from the bulk of the ore to the cold air whizzing past the train.

Bruce had the sides of the ore fleet sprayed with a 2-inch coating of polyurethane foam insulation and the decades-old frozen-ore problem was over.

CHAPTER 7

METAL FATIGUE

Bruce's tenure at U.S. Steel lasted five years. It had been spectacularly successful, but by 1964, he was beginning to feel that his outsider approach and research-driven focus was about to hit a wall. Despite his successes, both U.S. Steel and the Pennsylvania Railroad were huge corporate bureaucracies. The steel maker was steadily losing market share to nimbler foreign rivals and the domestic mini-mill industry, while the railroad was sleepwalking into oblivion as the new Interstate Highway System was funneling the most lucrative merchandise shipments from railroad boxcars to the fast-growing trucking industry. One young executive with a master's degree was not going to change that.

"I didn't realize it at the time," Bruce said, "but I was witnessing the first signs of fatigue in the great industrial machine that had

won two world wars and made America the most prosperous
nation in the world."

Trucking had its own unexamined problems

Bruce found his exit ramp in 1964, thanks once again to an academic. A professor at Michigan State University, Dr. Ed Smykay,
who was impressed with Bruce's quantitative analysis of transportation problems, reached out to him to ask whether he might be
interested in establishing a marketing department for an intercity
trucking company, the Chicago-based Spector Freight Systems.

"I had little formal training in marketing, but the money looked
good," Bruce said. The family moved to suburban Barrington
and Bruce began a daily commute to the Loop. When he left
U.S. Steel, he had taken with him some advice he had picked up
from Germane.

"Whenever you step into a new job or a new situation," the professor had told him, "be like a good bridge player and try to lay down
a couple of quick tricks before the other players realize what's happening. Remember, those fellows shaking your hand and smiling
at you are waiting for you to screw up. They want your job. If you
can show your boss on day one you know what you're talking
about you can de-fang the pretenders."

"It's freezing in here."

Bruce moved quickly. During his quick orientation on trucking-
industry practices, he learned that, during cold weather, a space
was left in the body of the semi-trailer for a charcoal heater
known as a "salamander" that was supposed to keep the lading
warm. The practice had been going on for decades—in fact, the

Interstate Commerce Commission had a rule that all wintertime truck and boxcar shipments had to be accompanied by either a charcoal salamander or an alcohol heater.

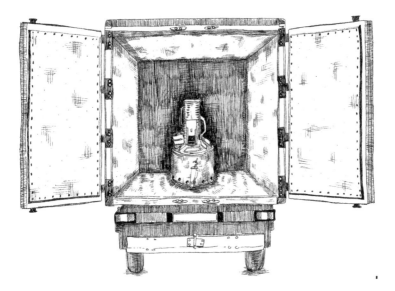

The salamanders aroused Bruce's suspicions.

"Any backyard barbecue chef knows charcoal burns away quickly," he said. "With no way to replenish the fuel supply, how long could the salamanders be expected to keep working?"

Fired by scientific curiosity, Bruce sent a couple of Spector trailers to the Budd Company for testing in the cryo-chamber and soon received a report confirming the charcoal heaters were virtually useless. Spector discontinued the devices, the ICC never found out, no shipper ever complained, the company banked a substantial saving, and potential rivals for Bruce's job were quieted.

Opening new lanes of commerce

Although Bruce had no formal training in marketing, his growing skills in quantitative analysis had arguably more of a business-building effect than a traditional marketing effort. In the still-regulated 1960s, the Interstate Commerce Commission required motor carriers seeking to enter a market to earn a Certificate of Necessity showing that shippers along a corridor needed an additional carrier to supply the capacity to move their goods. Bruce found Spector had those certificates for dozens of routes but was running trucks on only about 40% of the mileage it was certified to serve. Management believed there was not enough business out there to warrant another competitor, so Spector stayed on the sidelines.

Curious—and sometimes downright suspicious—Bruce applied a mathematical tool he had learned at UT to measure the potential market along those routes.

"My UT master's thesis had been titled, 'Spatial Relations and Economic Interaction,'" he said. "Its principles included a simple formula showing that if you knew the number of employees at a manufacturing facility and plugged in a couple of other standard numbers, you could derive the factory's annual output and, per corollary, its shipping needs."

In pre-internet days the only way to do that was to pore over each state's annual economic atlas. Bruce did, toting up all the factories in Michigan, Ohio, and New Jersey and their respective payrolls. The results told him there was business out there for Spector.

The trucking industry in the 1960s was not exactly famous for welcoming college grads into its ranks, but Bruce was more than a bright young guy with a slide rule. He also was an alumnus of the Army's public-speaker training and his presentations, along with the written documentation Tennessee had taught him to prepare, won the attention of Spector management. The carrier opened five new terminals in Michigan, three in Ohio, and three in New Jersey. From day one new traffic began to flow, and within six months it was clear that all of the new business was profitable.

CHAPTER 8

A HUNCH IS NOT ENOUGH

The Spector experience disclosed an important element in
Bruce's skill set: he was highly intuitive, but he never relied on
intuition alone to guide him toward a decision. He would allow
his intuition to point him toward the solution to a problem,
but he would not proceed until he had sufficient numerical
confirmation that his hunch had been right. "First get the
numbers" became his motto, and it never failed him. That
makeup math course at Rutgers had become the gift that kept
on giving.

Somehow, Bruce found time during his busy days at Spector to
continue teaching college business students about quantitative
solutions to industrial transportation problems. This time, his
forum was before the incoming graduate students at DePaul
University on the city's North Side.

Exploiting a railroad's weakness

If bright young college grads were rare in the trucking industry they were even harder to find at the railroads, where super-annuated "traffic officials" still performed their archaic sales-and-pricing rituals without the aid of contemporary marketing studies. His Pittsburgh days had convinced Bruce that the Pennsylvania Railroad was one of the sleepier carriers, so he approached its sales people to find out whether Spector might save money by shipping some of its trailers from Chicago to northern New Jersey on the Pennsylvania's premier "piggyback" train. Driver wages were high in the days of Jimmy Hoffa's reign over the Teamsters' Union, so having the trailers ride on railroad flatcars sounded like a promising way to cut costs.

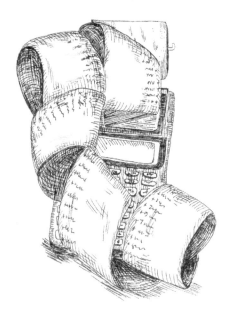

Bruce had no idea how drastic Spector's saving would be until he visited the Pennsylvania's traffic department in Philadelphia and learned how the railroad priced its Trailer On Flat Car (TOFC) business. Unlike the truck lines, which charged the shipper not just on the mileage but also on the value of the cargo, the clueless Pennsy had a flat rate of $200 on any trailer traveling between Chicago and New Jersey.

"It didn't matter whether the trailer contained $300,000 worth of jewelry or $3,000 worth of paper towels—the charge was a flat $200 per trailer," Bruce said. "That figure came right out of the mouth of Fred Carpi, the Pennsylvania's vice president of traffic. The price was so low I was about to ask, 'Wait a minute—are you sure? That number doesn't sound right.' Fortunately, I checked myself at the last moment and said something like, 'O.K., let me just write this down: It's $200 per trailer from Chicago to New Jersey, right?'"

Carpi nodded in confirmation.

Spector's cost for a highway move from Chicago to New Jersey was $350. Bruce didn't need a calculator to multiply the $150-per-trailer saving by the number of trailers Spector needed to move between Chicago and New Jersey each night. He immediately switched every Spector trailer he could find to Pennsy's piggyback train.

"Four years later," Bruce mused, "it crossed my mind that in my own little way I had helped catapult the Pennsylvania Railroad—by then the Penn Central—into the largest corporate bankruptcy in American history."

Soaked by a slosh in the suds

By that time, Bruce was off to his next corporate adventure, the Joseph Schlitz Brewery in Milwaukee. Once again, head hunters had learned about Bruce's skill in shaking up sleepy operations, and Schlitz was loaded with them. In 1967, the Bruce family moved to suburban Mequon, Wisconsin, and Bruce reported for work at the brewery, where he staged a quick repeat of his temperature successes at U.S. Steel and Spector.

Like Spector, Schlitz was trying to protect its wintertime loads of beer with alcohol heaters, only the product was being shipped in boxcars rather than semis. Bruce sent a couple of beer-filled boxcars and alcohol heaters to the Budd Company for testing and, sure enough, the same results came back as before—the heaters were useless. Since Schlitz owned 2,000 alcohol heaters, getting rid of all that hopeless hardware saved the company a ton of money, and Schlitz CEO Bobby Uihlein rewarded Bruce with a big chunk of stock.

Another clueless American industry

Thermal analyses didn't occupy Bruce for long. Schlitz had much bigger problems.

"As I visited the company's network of plants and talked with its managers and colleagues in the industry, I began to realize that Schlitz's owners were struggling ineffectually with new competitive pressures they didn't understand," he wrote.

A troublesome subsidiary of Schlitz in Belgium went bankrupt, the first U.S. company in Europe to do so. More adroit competitors in the U.S. were muscling in on markets that Schlitz had long deemed its "franchise." For the first time, foreign beers were becoming accepted in the U.S. market, snatching market share from bungling legacy brands like Schlitz.

Like the Pennsylvania Railroad and U.S. Steel, Schlitz was suffering from a sort of organizational fatigue. The company faltered fatally when it tried to juice its profits by using a new process that promised to reduce the beer's aging time.

"The old German brewmasters warned them that the innovation was dangerous, but management wouldn't listen," Bruce said. Sales went into a swoon as the customers switched to superior brands.

"I got out just before the end," Bruce said. "I should have sold that stock Uihlein gave me before it collapsed."

CHAPTER 9

THE CHANCE TO WORK
WITH A LEGEND

Bruce was rescued from the sinking ship by another executive
recruiter, Bob Reebie, who was reaching out with an offer Bruce
couldn't refuse—the chance to work not just for a railroad, but
for one of the railroad industry's few genuine heroes, Alfred E.
Perlman. While most U.S. railroad CEOs during the '50s and '60s
were presiding haplessly over money-losing industrial dinosaurs,
Perlman not only was rescuing doomed carriers but polishing
them up into money-making enterprises admired throughout
the industry.

His first railroad rehab was the Denver & Rio Grande Western, a
struggling Denver-Salt Lake City "bridge" carrier. As D&RGW's
executive vice-president during the early 1950s, Perlman saved
the company from bankruptcy by replacing an army of track

laborers with modern machinery and by scrapping the company's aging steam locomotives in favor of more economical diesels.

Perlman's feats at the Rio Grande caught the attention of the ailing, 9,000-mile New York Central, the famed offspring of the Vanderbilt family that stretched from Boston and New York to Chicago and St. Louis.

Installed as president in 1954, Perlman slashed long-term debt by $100 million, ruthlessly discontinuing money-losing passenger trains, ripping out the two main tracks they used on the company's 4-track main line between Albany and Buffalo, and automating the carrier's largest freight yards—Albany, Buffalo, Indianapolis, and Elkhart, Indiana. Industry experts had predicted a New York Central bankruptcy. Perlman turned the carrier into a money maker. He also made the New York Central into a sort of graduate school for training railroad managers, where only the best and brightest got to attend Perlman's master classes.

Can Perlman's magic save the Western Pacific?

Now he was at it again. A Philadelphia financier named Mickey Newman had acquired control of the Western Pacific, a small railroad that operated 927 miles of single-track main line between Oakland and Salt Lake City, where it connected with Perlman's alma mater, the Rio Grande. The Western Pacific had been built by local entrepreneurs in the early 20th century to give shippers an alternative to the giant Union Pacific/Southern Pacific/Chicago & North Western combine, the so-called "Overland Route" that had enjoyed a monopoly on travel and shipping between Chicago and San Francisco. Through an alliance with the Rio Grande and the Burlington Route, Western Pacific offered a parallel alternative between Oakland and Chicago.

When Newman hired Perlman to helm the WP in August of 1970, things were not going well for the scrappy little railroad. The Interstate highway system was stealing the rail industry's most profitable traffic—consumer-merchandise shipments. Bruce arrived and became the VP of marketing and started finding opportunities the previous management had overlooked.

His opening act was one that had become habitual—boxcar heating. Unlike Schlitz and Spector, the WP may not have been using salamanders, but it was using alcohol heaters suspended from the car ceilings. Bruce was mind-boggled at the practice. Since heat rises, how was heat generated at the top of the car supposed to reach cargo stored underneath it? This time, there were no tests needed in the cryo chamber. Bruce simply showed Perlman and WP President Mike Flannery the lab reports that ended car heating at Spector and Schlitz, and, after a brief conference, they ordered WP's heaters discontinued.

If you can't beat 'em, join 'em: the railroad becomes a truck line
Never content to rest on his laurels, Bruce parlayed his trucking
experience into another coup. Like many railroads, the WP was
carrying a growing volume of "piggyback" traffic as shippers
tried to save money by putting their semi-trailers on railroad
flatcars. The WP's problem was that virtually all of its piggyback
shipments were westbound. Once the trailers were unloaded in
Oakland, they were returned to Denver and Chicago empty,
depriving WP of a potentially robust revenue stream.

Using his UT training, once again, Bruce did a survey of Bay
Area shippers to identify eastbound semi-trailers that had loads
in them. He found plenty. The question was, how to get them off
the highway and onto the Western Pacific? Bruce's answer was
simple–have the WP form its own truck line, send sales people
out to solicit traffic, and leverage the lower cost of piggybacking to
send the trailers east on flatcars.

Bruce's colleagues immediately protested. Didn't the Interstate
Commerce Commission have a rule against railroads owning
their own truck lines? Bruce checked the regulations and found
the WP marketing staff was misinformed. The ICC did have a rule
against railroads going into the trucking business if they used the
trucks in intercity service parallel to their own tracks, but if the
railroad used its trucks strictly for local pickup and delivery to
bring shipments to its trains, the ICC had no objection.

We're gonna be truckers now (but first we go to school)
Bruce had the company's lawyers charter a WP trucking company
and hired a veteran trucking executive to run it. Before launching
the new operation, he conducted an after-hours "school" to teach
the trucking executives about railroading and the WP traffic

officers about truck economics. Having worked in both industries, he knew the two did not understand each other, and, having
polished his persuasive skills at Murder Board, he knew how to
persuade a roomful of skeptics into pulling together as a team.

Bruce's short course turned out to be popular. The staff actually
enjoyed the lessons and emerged highly enthusiastic about the
initiative. Once everybody was on the same page, Bruce booked
space at a local cross-dock warehouse, and every evening, a couple
of WP trucks would come off the streets with shipments for the
East and Midwest that they had collected during the day. The
trucks would back up to the dock and, after sorting, the shipments would be transferred onto piggyback trailers that were
waiting on the other side of the dock. A couple of hours later, the
trailers would be loaded on an eastbound piggyback train at WP's
Oakland yard.

From an initial two warehouse doors, WP was soon backing its
trucks up to eleven doors each day. WP piggyback trains were
now running east with almost as many revenue-earning loads as
the westbounds.

Turnaround time at the little WP: It's real

When Perlman had arrived at the WP in December 1970, its
accountants had forecast an annual loss of $14 million and
the bank account held only $259,000—enough for one payroll.
Thanks to Perlman's ruthless cost cutting and Bruce's aggressive
marketing, the scrappy little company turned in a 1971 profit of
$3.9 million.

There was one more mountain to climb. Every railroad executive
with any ambition falls asleep each night dreaming of getting a

big shipper to locate a major facility on the railroad's line. Once a shipper builds a facility with a rail siding, all of its business goes to the railroad whose tracks serve the plant. While publicly owned highways enable any shipper to be served by multiple motor carriers, rail shippers can use only the railroad that enters their property. The more shippers who locate a facility on a railroad, the more carloads that railroad carries.

Find that lucky Penney

Early in 1974, Western Pacific learned that it was facing just such an opportunity. JCPenney & Co. disclosed that it was planning to build a giant new Western distribution warehouse—the largest in the retail-merchandising industry at that time—in Reno, Nevada. If that warehouse were built at a site along WP's tracks, the little railroad would enjoy booming revenues as the Western economy continued to grow and its population continued to turn to Penney's for clothing, footwear, kitchen utensils, appliances, carpeting, toys, and furniture.

There was just one problem–competition. Reno was served by two railroads, the WP and its historic rival, the rich and rascally Southern Pacific. SP usually won these contests, but Bruce had a hunch he could outfox the old dinosaur.

Discretion is the better part of valor (and sales)

His first move was to quietly secure an option on a large piece of property in Reno served by a WP siding. SP of course had a tract of its own a few miles away. It was a long shot. SP had a history of winning big contests, but Bruce was determined and hopeful. He took Penney executives out to the site in WP's luxurious business car and arranged for them to survey the site from a chartered helicopter, but Southern Pacific had a whole train of business cars and a budget for steak dinners and golf outings that WP could not match.

There was an outside chance for WP, however. As the contest approached its conclusion, Penney's made it clear to both contestants that the company would not tolerate any premature disclosure of its decision. Penney's feared any leak about the new warehouse would set off a surge of property speculation in the area around the site and Penney's would be blamed for the ensuing rise in property prices. The penalty for a premature disclosure was severe. Penney's warned that if either side blabbed prior to Penney's announcement, the other would get the award.

Bruce had always been an intuitive type, sniffing out opportunities where others saw nothing. From his post in San Francisco, Bruce asked the Reno sales office to keep an eye on the SP people. They were known to be arrogant, cocksure, and sometimes indiscreet. Sure enough, Bruce's Reno sales manager, Ken Plummer, called Bruce with some news. At a customer dinner the night before in a Reno restaurant, an SP salesman couldn't help whispering that Penney's had made its choice. The warehouse would be built on SP's site. Then Plummer dropped a second bomb. One of the dinner guests was a reporter who planned to run a story about JCPenney's decision in the local paper the next morning.

"Get two copies of that paper and get on a flight to New York," Bruce instructed Plummer, who at first didn't understand. "Don't worry about the air fare—I'll authorize it. Just get yourself a ticket on the first flight to New York and bring two copies of that paper with you. I'm leaving now and I'll meet you there and explain."

The two men rendezvoused in New York. The puzzled Plummer handed over the newspapers and returned to Reno while Bruce retired to a hotel to polish his plot and catch some sleep. Ever since his performances before the Murder Board, Bruce had understood that he needed to present information in the most appealing and, if necessary, dramatic manner. Now he put his scheme into action.

Knowing that JCPenney's Director of Catalog Operations, Ralph Henderson, always arrived at company headquarters at the same time each morning and always stopped to buy a newspaper before enjoying coffee and a cigar in the building's coffee shop, Bruce got out of a cab in front of 1301 Avenue of the Americas just in time to ambush Henderson on the sidewalk.

"Harry Bruce—what are you doing here?" said Henderson.

"Let's go up to your office and I'll tell you all about it."

The pair mumbled small talk as the elevator rose to the 43rd floor, then streamed past Henderson's puzzled secretary and entered his office. Henderson shut the door and with a suspicious smile playing about his lips asked, "Now, what is this all about?"

Bruce whipped out a copy of the Reno paper and held it, front-page forward, in front of Henderson's baffled face.

"Your morning paper, sir," he announced in his best English-butler delivery.

"Give me that," Henderson said, snatching the paper, bounding out the door and heading down the corridor to the right. Bruce knew from the direction Henderson took that he was heading straight to the office of Penney's president, Walter Neppl.

Henderson returned a few minutes later and told Bruce, "You got the business."

Bruce's triumph was complete. When he returned to San Francisco and briefed WP's top management, he was a hero. "Perlman could hardly contain his delight," Bruce said. The crusty, demanding, imperious boss immediately awarded him a bonus check for $2,500.

"I still don't understand how it all happened," Bruce said. "It seemed like there must have been some kind of witch doctor at work. I was in that special region of bliss reserved for the small army of railroad men who had pleased Alfred E. Perlman."

CHAPTER 10

PERLMAN AND THE
MYSTERY OF LEADERSHIP

Pleasing Perlman was a heady experience for Bruce, but it also left
him wondering why he had worked so hard and dared so lavishly
in order to please this difficult man in the first place. Based on
his record, Perlman was a great leader. He had now rescued three
written-off railroads and become, not just an industry legend,
but an American business icon. Yet Perlman's personal treatment
of his subordinates sometimes defied many of the rules in the
leadership books.

If a subordinate failed to perform, Perlman would dress them
down in front of their peers, a practice frowned upon in all of the
leadership literature. The authorities agreed that any unfavorable
performance review should be conducted in private, but Perlman
had become infamous for his "balloon ascensions" in which first
his neck, then his face, would turn purple while he held up a

failing manager to ridicule as his embarrassed peers stared at their shoes.

"For a successful corporate manager and global thinker, Perlman could be incredibly petty and fussy." Bruce said. On a business-car inspection trip across the Nevada desert, Perlman suddenly ordered the train stopped and backed up because he had noticed that a signal mast had been painted the wrong color.

"Who painted that signal mast silver?" Perlman roared at the vice-president of communications and signals. "Everybody knows the signal masts on this railroad are supposed to be black! What kind of organization are you and your people running here when people can just go out and slop a bucket of silver paint on a signal mast just because they feel like it? I want you to go out and find the guy who did that and—and—"

Bruce said the episode was "like Captain Queeg with the straw-berries". Some of the executives on the car were so unnerved that they left the halted business car and took a short walk in the desert to avoid Perlman's tantrum. Fortunately, the tempest was quelled when WP President Mike Flannery, a favorite Perlman brought with him from the New York Central, said, "All right, Mr. Perlman, let's stop it right now. The signal will be repainted on Monday and there won't be a repetition of that mistake. All our signals will be black and they'll stay black."

Flannery's appeal took the wind out of Perlman's sails and the inspection trip resumed, but the experience only left Bruce pondering the mysteries of leadership—how could a man capable of such pettiness be such a spectacularly successful business leader?

Even Perlman's victims acknowledged their respect for him and tried to please him, and many succeeded. Why, Bruce wanted to know. What exactly was leadership, and how did it work?

That question would pester Bruce even as he rose to a leadership position.

The recruiters prowl

Bruce's coup with the JCPenney project caught the attention of corporate headhunters. In the spring of 1975, the phone began to ring with offers, including one from the Illinois Central Gulf Railroad in Chicago. Would Bruce consider becoming the ICG's vice president of marketing?

Despite his devotion to Perlman, Bruce agreed to come to Chicago for an interview. Few serious marketing challenges remained for Bruce at WP, but for an executive seeking bigger challenges there were still plenty at larger, older, and troubled carriers like the ICG, and ICG CEO Alan Boyd knew his company had big problems. When Bruce announced his salary demands, Boyd briefly boggled, but then agreed. Since all ICG vice-presidents earned an identical or lesser amount, Bruce had to be given a bigger title—senior vice president of marketing.

Bigger railroad, bigger problems

The challenge was the biggest Bruce had ever faced. The Illinois Central Gulf was the product of a 1972 merger between the historic Illinois Central, launched in 1854 as Chicago's connection with New Orleans; and the Gulf, Mobile & Ohio, a collection of weaker regional lines merged over the years into a single carrier that, like the IC, linked Chicago to the Gulf of Mexico. Unlike the IC, however, the GM&O's trains rambled over a series of ill-matched regional routes that missed several important cities and never earned enough revenue to keep the tracks up to standard. Many of the GM&O routes were duplicates of the IC's, and all but the busiest main lines were so under-maintained that derailments occurred almost daily. The railroad was a mess.

What kind of a corporation is this?

As poor as its routes and track may have been, the biggest challenge of all was ICG's ownership structure. ICG was not a standalone railroad but a troubled component of a sprawling, hard to manage "conglomerate" known as IC Industries—or simply "Industries" in management-speak. During the 1960s and '70s, much of American industry embraced a business school fad that claimed profits would best be protected if corporations were organized as holding companies made up of components from totally unrelated industries. It was basically a hedging strategy—if one or two of the components experienced a loss of market share or a drop in profits, the trouble would be offset by growth in the healthier holdings. IC Industries' management felt the best role for the railroad was to sell off or develop its vast trove of surplus real estate so that Industries could use the proceeds to buy healthier companies. No growth strategy or profit targets for the railroad itself had been developed.

In addition to all of its other troubles, Illinois Central Gulf Railroad had to compete for corporate attention and capital against the conglomerate's other holdings, such as a Pepsi-Cola bottling company, the Midas Muffler chain, the Abex brake-shoe manufacturing company, and Huffman Corp., a manufacturer of commercial refrigeration equipment. How did a huge, sprawling, money-losing railroad fit into the mix?

The railroad was a wreck

The ICG was in a precarious state when Bruce agreed to join the company. The Interstate highway network had been completed, and shippers were closing their rail sidings and switching to trucks. Business was hemorrhaging from the secondary and branch lines, where short-haul traffic proved particularly vulnerable to trucking. The Chicago-New Orleans main line was busy, but the company lacked the resources to maintain the track, and derailments had become increasingly common—and dangerous. The ICG booked a third of its revenues from an 80-mile single-track branch between Baton Rouge and New Orleans that served more than 60 large chemical plants, and the tank cars filled with toluene, glycerine, naphtha, and other valuable chemicals represented the ICG's largest and most reliable source of profits. As the main line continued to deteriorate due to a lack of maintenance, more and more of these cars derailed and blew up, leading to expensive lawsuits and settlements with property owners and local communities.

"What is the plan?"

The most serious problem at the ICG was managerial paralysis. Top management seemed unable to understand what was happening to the railroad or what to do about it. The GM&O merger had left the Illinois Central Gulf with over 9,000 miles of track—more than the giant New York Central—but without the carloadings or ton-miles to support the huge physical plant. What was to be done with all that idle track and the more than 21,000 employees, more than two employees per mile, much greater than the industry standard?

As senior vice president of marketing, Bruce had no jurisdiction over the vast mass of operating employees, but he knew there was plenty of excess employment in his own small department. Driving from Oakland to his new office in Chicago, he stopped in to check out the railroad's off-line sales offices in Salt Lake City, Denver, Omaha, and Des Moines, and as he suspected, they were obsolete, developing barely enough business to pay the sales staff's salary and the office rent.

The sales staff weren't building any new business, instead, they were simply taking a dwindling number of orders from a dwindling number of shippers. Before he reached Chicago, Bruce had closed all the offices. They were producing nothing and the ICG management hadn't even noticed.

Hank Davenport, Bruce's unexpected gift

Shortly after Bruce arrived at the ICG, the CEO who had hired him retired, leaving Bruce without a corporate "sponsor" and vulnerable to rivals seeking his job, but the job was so thankless that no one else wanted it, so no rivals emerged. The new CEO, ICG's Washington lobbyist Bill Taylor, did not know Bruce and apparently had no plans for marketing, so Bruce was left alone to develop his own marketing strategy.

Taylor did present Bruce with one valuable gift, however. When he moved to Chicago from Washington, he brought with him his assistant, Hank Davenport, a veteran ICG operating official who knew the railroad from the ballast up. Bruce and Davenport took an immediate liking to each other. As their friendship deepened, Davenport would invite Bruce to join him on the office car when he went out on inspection trips, and he eagerly shared all of his knowledge about how the railroad operated, where the trains ran, what they carried, how much revenue they earned or lost, and which officials were responsible for the main lines, the branches, the yards, and the repair shops that kept the business running. The business-car trips with Davenport were like a master class in railroad operations. Always an eager student, Bruce imbibed all the details Davenport shared with him and quickly accumulated a portfolio of facts, numbers, contacts, and insight that most executives develop only over years of experience. Formally just a marketing executive, Bruce was becoming a stealth operating "official." He was learning how the ICG worked.

Talk the talk until you learn to walk the walk
Bruce now combined Davenport's gift of system familiarization with an earlier gift of his own.

"My second piece of good luck was finding I had a hidden talent I could use to convince my superiors I was indispensable—the public-speaking skills I had picked up in the Army," Bruce said.

"And boy, did the ICG need a public speaker," he said. "Financially challenged as it was, the company had to make periodic presentations on its business prospects to the investment-rating services— Moody's, Standard & Poor's, Fitch and Value Line."

The problem was, most ICG managers couldn't make a decent presentation. Discovering Bruce's talent for making clear, convincing presentations, management started sending him along to these events, as well as on visits to shippers, shipper-trade associations, and local economic-development authorities. All of them had been desperately awaiting some sort of reassurance from the ICG, and now Bruce was providing it.

Bruce's presentations weren't just hype. Although deregulation would not arrive until 1980, IC Industries' brilliant chief financial officer, John Fagen, another Perlman alumnus from the New York Central turnaround and a Beltway insider, assured Bruce and the industry analysts that a major legislative effort was under way in Washington. This push would finally relieve the railroads of their onerous federal regulations and let them compete toe-to-toe with the truckers and the barge industry.

Even though deregulation was several years in the future, Bruce was able to assure the analysts that another piece of good news was coming sooner. In 1976, Congress passed the Railroad Revitalization and Regulatory Reform (4-R) Act, which set aside several billion dollars in low-interest loans to enable the railroads to rebuild their crumbling infrastructure. In 1977, the first funds became available and ICG qualified for $167 million worth of assistance. The loans came with strings—recipient railroads had to issue "preference shares" to the federal government so if a loan were not paid back, the government ended up owning a piece of the railroad.

The ICG never paid that penalty. It rebuilt the entire double-track main line from Chicago to New Orleans, repaid the government, and enjoyed a long-overdue dividend—no more derailments. The tank cars stopped blowing up, the lawsuits ended, and ICG's insurance premiums sank back to tolerable levels. With the trains running on time, Bruce's team could get out and sell more rail transportation to more shippers.

"You can't sell from an empty wagon"

Selling was what Bruce had been hired to do, and Bruce and his team devised a number of innovative ways to use the less-than-ideal railroad network at their disposal.

Truck-Rail-Truck

Coiled sheet steel—the kind used by auto and appliance manufacturers—earns high freight rates when hauled by train and even higher rates when hauled by truck, but the trucks were making away with most of the business because they could drive straight from the steel mill to the customer overnight. The same shipment on a railroad car had to be picked up from the mill by a switching railroad, then taken to a nearby yard and classified into a train destined for an ICG yard, then hauled to the ICG yard, then reclassified in the ICG's yard into an ICG train headed for a yard near the customer, and then switched into another train serving the customer's siding. Rail shipping was a lot cheaper than trucking, but it was a lot slower too. Time being money, the customers were going with trucks.

Bruce's team devised a better way by developing a dolly that could move a giant coil of steel off a flatbed truck without using a crane. The truck would load at a Gary, Indiana steel mill, drive to the IC's Markham yard outside Chicago, and discharge the coil right onto an IC flatcar scheduled to leave that same night, eliminating the two-day railcar switching shuffle. A day later at Memphis or two days later at New Orleans or Mobile, the reverse process transferred the steel coil from the railcar to a local truck headed straight for the customer's factory. The customers saved thousands of dollars compared to over-the-road trucking and rewarded the ICG with a growing line of business.

"Slingshot" intermodal trains

In its merger with the GM&O, the Illinois Central had acquired the latter's 285-mile Chicago-St. Louis main line. Bruce now moved to exploit it, offering truck shippers a cheaper way to get their trailers of expedited merchandise between the two cities. Three daily piggyback trains—known as "Slingshots"—whisked the trailers across the Illinois prairie in about eight hours at a cost well below what the motor carriers were charging. Margins on the business were slim because the unions still required a full 5-man train crew, but the ICG's rates were still attractive enough to attract lots of business. At one point, a large bakery in Chicago used the Slingshots to supply buns to all the McDonald's outlets in the St. Louis area.

"The phantom five feet"

Bruce's experience at Spector and Western Pacific had left him suspicious about the piggyback-trailer business. Customers didn't always understand the concept of shipping truck trailers on railroad flatcars, and railroad executives didn't seem to understand it either. One problem was the trucking industry itself. Motor carriers had begun ordering longer trailers, stretching the conventional trailer from 40 to 45 feet, and so now railroad piggyback shippers were starting to demand that the railroads supply them with these longer trailers.

Bruce was suspicious. Did ICG's shippers really need that extra length? Did the cash-strapped railroad really need to replace its otherwise satisfactory 40-foot trailers with expensive new 45-foot models? Or was the "demand" for 45-footers simply a fad pursued by shippers who didn't know how to use the space in the trailers the railroad was supplying to them?

Bruce had a hunch that the shippers didn't understand their own needs and once again his mathematical experience told him to "get the numbers." He hired a consultant to take a random sample of 800 ICG trailers moving between New Orleans and Chicago to find out how full they were. The consultant started opening the doors of trailers arriving in Chicago and found out that scarcely any customers needed a 45-foot trailer—most came nowhere near to filling the 40-footers. ICG did order a few new 45-foot trailers for customers who genuinely needed them, but Bruce saved the railroad several million dollars by keeping the old 40-foot trailers running instead of retiring them prematurely.

Spreading the word they didn't want to hear

Bruce couldn't keep his mouth shut about his discovery and began trumpeting his numbers to his colleagues at other railroads. At a meeting of the Intermodal Association of North America in Atlanta, he delivered a speech entitled "The Phantom Five Feet: What Railroads Don't Know about Their Intermodal Shippers and What It's Doing to the Bottom Line". The speech was not widely applauded, nor was the pocket-sized reprint that Bruce circulated around the industry. The managerial ego does not enjoy having its weaknesses exposed, and for several years afterward, Bruce endured frosty glances and chilly handshakes from industry peers.

Regardless, for the ICG, the exposure of the Phantom Five Feet paid off handsomely. ICG sales people spent more time with their customers identifying how much space shipments actually needed and training the shippers' dock personnel in how to configure shipments for the most economical use of trailer space. The shippers appreciated the attention and tendered more business.

Rotten meat

Marketing isn't the same as sales, i.e., getting more business. Sometimes marketing means getting rid of business you already have because it just doesn't pay anymore. Bruce did that when he

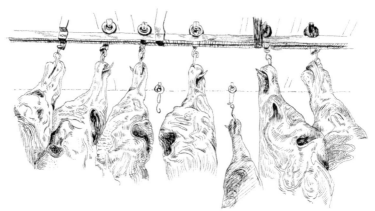

ended a venerable and treasured product line: carrying freshly slaughtered sides of fresh beef, pork, and lamb from slaughterhouses in Omaha, Sioux City, and Sioux Falls to Chicago in refrigerated boxcars.

The fault wasn't the ICG's. By the mid-1970s, the logistics of the meat packing industry were changing in ways entirely out of the railroad's control. Thanks to improvements in refrigeration and highway transportation, slaughtering no longer had to be concentrated in giant urban facilities served by rail sidings. Smaller slaughterhouses now were springing up out in the countryside right next to the feedlots where the animals were raised, and better highways enabled farmers to deliver small batches of animals to a local slaughterhouse after a short drive.

The packing houses had changed too—they no longer shipped whole sides of cattle or pigs to the city to be portioned into smaller cuts by butchers. The major supermarket chains wanted their meat pre-cut into steaks, chops, roasts, and even cubes for stewing, eliminating the local butcher from the supply chain and moving the entire meat-portioning process into the countryside.

When meat slaughtered in Iowa and Nebraska headed east in the form of halves and quarters suspended from the ceiling of a refrigerator car by meat hooks, the Illinois Central Railroad had been the king of the "swingin' meat" business. Each night a solid train of refrigerator cars headed to Chicago on a passenger-train timetable, but by the mid-70s, the business was dwindling as pre-portioned meat destined for a myriad of local supermarkets switched from train to truck. The few carloads the ICG was still carrying were losing money.

Bruce naturally pondered eliminating the swingin' meat business, but he didn't make his decision until his research showed him just how rotten it was.

"The few packers still shipping swingin' meat on the ICG were basically gaming the system," he said. "They wouldn't ship by rail unless they knew the meat was going bad. When the shipment arrived spoiled, the shipper's customer would file a claim against the railroad, and after we paid the claim the customer would split the take with the packer. Once I learned what was happening, I shut the whole meat business down and sold off all our refrigerator cars."

CHAPTER 11
SCHOOL DAYS

Increasingly impressed with Bruce, ICG management in mid-1979 enrolled him in Harvard Business School's Advanced Management Program for 16 weeks of intensive study. Bruce lived in Baker Hall with the incoming class of professional business managers, took his meals with them in Kresge Hall, attended lectures with the school's world-famous faculty and spent his evenings reading through the course materials, writing essays, and preparing for some of academia's most rigorous exams.

He also earned some extra credit. Harvard had supplied each dorm room with a small bookcase and assorted titles for discretionary reading. One of the volumes, *Small is Beautiful*, by E.M. Schumacher, caught Bruce's eye. It had been a best-seller during the 1970s, but Bruce had been too busy to read it. Now he did, and its arguments immediately resonated. Yes, giant corporations enjoyed many advantages in the way they used resources such as capital, labor, land, fuel, and transportation, but their very size made them clumsy and hard to maneuver in the search for new markets, new products, new ideas, and new talent. Bruce had seen big railroads fail exactly as Schumacher had predicted. The more he read, the more he realized something his superiors didn't want to hear–the Illinois Central Gulf Railroad needed to be smaller.

Schumacher was not the only breakthrough thinker who appealed to Bruce during his Harvard break. The 1973 OPEC oil embargo had awakened the nation to the increasing peril of dependency on fossil fuels, so Bruce decided to bring himself up to speed by reading Daniel Yergin and Robert Stobaugh's 1979 book, *Energy Future*. While most contemporary readers focused on the chapters dealing with petroleum, Bruce wanted to know what the authors thought about the prospects for coal.

Black diamonds losing glitter
Historically, the ICG–and particularly its IC component–had carried a lot of coal. Its main line sliced right through the heart of the soft-coal belt in southern Illinois and western Kentucky, and, for generations, IC trains had supplied the fuel that heated Chicago's homes and powered its industries. As homes and businesses increasingly switched to natural gas for heating and as the big steel mills in Chicago and Gary contracted, the railroad was carrying less of this once-profitable traffic. Most ICG coal now was being burned only in electrical generating stations.

Further aggravating the situation was the 1973 Clean Air Act, which mandated that electric generating stations had to mix their supplies of high-sulfur coal–the kind the ICG carried–with a

certain percentage of low-sulfur coal. Two railroads, the Chicago
& North Western and the Burlington Northern, already had
built extensions into Wyoming's Powder River basin to bring the
environmentally compliant mineral to Chicago. The ICG's high-
sulfur coal from southern Illinois and western Kentucky seemed
obsolete. Could that trend be reversed?

Academia engaged

Although Yergin and Stobaugh's book focused largely on oil, it did
contain a chapter on coal written by a brilliant young Harvard
economist named Mel Horwitch. Bruce called him and asked him
over to talk. Horwitch, intrigued that a businessman was reaching out to him, came over to Bruce's dorm dressed in sweat gear
from his morning run. Their meeting ignited a small marketing
revolution in the railroad industry.

When Bruce returned to Chicago at the end of 1979, he engaged
Horwitch to assist the ICG with some of the most intense and
rigorous marketing studies ever conducted by a North American
railroad—a survey of the entire global coal market to identify
which countries and industries used coal, what types of coal
they needed, where they were sourcing it and, most importantly,
whether mines on the ICG could supply it at a competitive price.

If the U.S. was rejecting high-sulfur coal, the rest of the world
still wanted it and Bruce wanted to know whether ICG could
deliver it. ICG, after all, was an exporting railroad, connecting
the Midwest and mid-South with the deepwater ports of New
Orleans, Gulfport, and Mobile. Bruce wanted to know what the
numbers said about using those ports to ship Illinois Basin coal to
different global destinations.

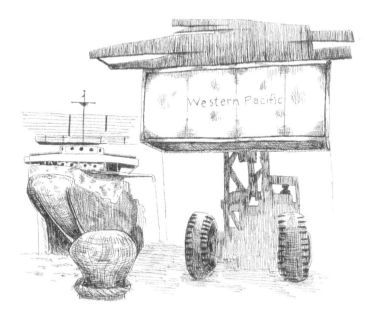

The result was ICG's *World Coal Guide*, published in 1981 in four languages, with maps documenting each type of coal the Illinois Basin produced, the industries worldwide that needed it, and the global shipping routes serving the ICG ports of New Orleans, Gulfport, and Mobile. Nothing like the *Guide* had ever before been issued by a railroad, an ocean carrier, or the coal industry.

Later that year, Horwitch's colleague, Professor Pedro Nueño of the IESE University in Barcelona, tipped Horwitch that Illinois Basin coal might work in the Spanish cement industry. Meetings with Spanish officials confirmed that the Illinois mineral was ideal for heating cement kilns, and soon the first shiploads were underway from the Port of Mobile. Later, the Greek cement industry became a customer, and the ships began loading at New Orleans.

The Illinois Basin coal industry was delighted. No railroad had ever displayed such leadership or worked so hard to help them market their product. ICG's marketing surpassed their own in depth and sophistication.

"The effect of the *World Coal Guide* on the ICG was striking," Bruce said. "Few people believed that an American railroad was capable of—or even interested in—performing the kind of professional marketing study normally associated with high-profile industries such as retailing or electronics or fast food. The effect on ICG employee morale was electric, and the front office at Industries noticed too."

CHAPTER 12

"LET THE DEREGULATION BEGIN"

The business world had yet to see just how imaginative and dynamic the ICG could be. As the 1970s came to a close, the railroad industry and its customers were approaching a watershed moment, the long-awaited prospect of deregulation. For the first time since the Interstate Commerce Commission was established in 1876—and particularly since Congress passed the Hepburn Act in 1906—all railroads doing business in the United States had to submit their rates for carrying each commodity to the ICC for approval and had to publish their rates so that all customers knew exactly how much a railroad was charging its other customers for carrying each commodity. There were no discounts for handling larger volumes and no private deals. All railroads were required to have their rates approved by the ICC and had to charge the same rates to all customers.

Originally necessary to make railroad rates transparent and fair, regulation turned out in practice to have a dangerous downside—it left railroads uninterested in pricing their product effectively. Knowing their competitors would be charging the same rates, the railroads had no incentive to identify their costs, or to explore ways of reducing them, or to make their company more attractive to a shipper. The typical railroad sales department was staffed not by actual salesmen but by clerks who looked up rates in a giant book and quoted them to the customers.

Perhaps worst of all, many railroads had grown comfortable with regulation and had never explored the benefits of operating in a deregulated, competitive environment. When this writer, then working as a transportation reporter, asked a Burlington Northern publicist in 1979, "What do you guys think about this deregulation that's coming?" the BN man answered, "We can live with it." Despite having advocated for deregulation, some of the Class 1 carriers were not ready for its arrival.

Bruce was. Having worked for both railroads and unregulated companies, he saw deregulation as a plus, at least for those who understood it and knew how to exploit it.

"The price is right"
Exploit it he did.

In October 1980, President Jimmy Carter signed the Staggers Deregulation Act, the third in a series of bills that deregulated first the airline industry, then long-distance trucking, and finally railroads. While welcoming deregulation, the airline and trucking moguls had moved hesitantly in adjusting their rates and their marketing approaches to the new market freedoms. When railroad deregulation came at last, most of the carriers were hesitant as well.

Not Bruce. He had his strategy ready well in advance and already had met quietly with dozens of customers to let them know they would soon be able to negotiate privately with the ICG for rate-and-service packages that made the most sense for both parties. Virtually all of ICG's customers welcomed their new freedoms and the clear and concise way that Bruce was explaining them, and they began to meet with ICG marketing representatives to negotiate their first contracts for rail transportation.

Within days of Carter's signature, Bruce sat down with the chairman of Hoosier Energy Corp. and the Freeman-United Coal Mining Co. and signed the first private contract executed between a shipper and a railroad carrying that shipper's commodity. Over a 20-year period, the ICG would carry coal from a Freeman

United mine in Macoupin County, Illinois, to a Hoosier Energy generating plant in Merom, Indiana, at a rate neither party would disclose.

Sensitive to symbolism, Bruce arranged for the pact to be signed beside an ICG coal train positioned on a viaduct carrying ICG's tracks over a street in Bloomington, Indiana. It was the first of forty such rate-and-service packages ICG would sign with its customers in the next few months. No other railroad was moving into the deregulated environment at such a pace.

"For the first time in decades the ICG was a leader at something," Bruce recalled. "The industry actually was watching us for signals. Some of them probably were waiting for us to fail, but it never happened."

CHAPTER 13

TWO FATAL—AND FATEFUL—
HEART ATTACKS

Deregulation—and Bruce's prompt and eager exploitation of it—had been exciting for everyone at the ICG, but Bruce also approached the date with a lingering pang of regret. A year before deregulation became law, his friend Hank Davenport had died of a heart attack while on a Mediterranean vacation with his wife.

"The ICG lost a first-class operating man, while I had lost a friend who had done so much to bridge the railroad industry's historic gap between the operating people and the marketing people," Bruce wrote.

If Bruce had moved so confidently toward deregulation while the industry giants dithered, Davenport was one of the reasons why. Because of him, Bruce knew all of the ICG's strengths and weaknesses. ICG still needed to be smaller—much smaller—in both track miles and employees, but inside of its sprawling map Bruce could see the bones of a real railroad if only IC Industries management could be persuaded that downsizing was the only way to go.

On Friday, April 15, 1983, while lunching with colleagues at the Chicago Club, Bruce was called to the phone and told that CEO Bill Taylor had collapsed while lunching at the Chicago Athletic Association. Bruce raced to Northwestern Memorial Hospital just in time to learn that Taylor had died.

ICG adrift

Neither the railroad nor the parent company had a succession plan. None of Taylor's vice presidents had been designated as successor, nor was there a strategy for seeking a successor from outside the company. Weeks passed, but no executive search firm was engaged. Instead, IC Industries CEO William Johnson called ICG's vice-presidents into his office for one-on-one interviews. Eventually, he worked his way down to Bruce and asked him the same question he'd asked the other candidates:

"Harry, what would you do with the ICG if you were CEO?"

"I had my answer ready," Bruce recalls. "It was not tailored to what I thought Johnson wanted to hear because I didn't know what Johnson wanted to hear. I simply told him what I believed:

"This railroad has never had a strategic business plan. I would immediately begin developing one, and I would insist that each department prepare its own plan. I would establish a three-year plan and update it annually."

Johnson listened but he did not signal whether he embraced or rejected Bruce's answer. Instead, he drilled down further:

"What kinds of elements would be in the plan?" Johnson asked.

"We need to plan what markets we want to be in and which ones we want to be out of," Bruce said. "Right now we're running certain kinds of trains and carrying certain kinds of freight just because we've always done it. I want to find out what's worth carrying and what's not, and I want us to be able to document numerically which lines of business are worth pursuing. This means we have to start studying our costs. We don't understand our costs, so we don't know which efforts are worth an invest-ment. We must justify every dollar, and we must develop a plan for how we're going to finance our projects. This will require a personnel plan as well: What kinds of people will we need to execute the plan? Where will we get them and how will we train them?"

"That's quite a program."

"Well, Mr. Johnson, I once heard you tell the board of directors that your father used to say, 'Plan your work and work your plan.' That always sounded good to me."

Johnson nodded but did not signal a response otherwise. Shortly after, Bruce was summoned to Johnson's office and told the board had elected him to be the new president, chairman, and chief executive officer of the Illinois Central Gulf Railroad.

Getting down to work

Although IC Industries did not have a formal corporate plan, it did have an agenda—sell the ICG. The parent company had already sold most of the railroad's surplus real estate and rolled the profits over into purchasing other businesses, so the railroad no longer had a meaningful role in IC Industries's portfolio.

The parent company's campaign to sell the ICG had not been successful. Several of the other Class 1 carriers had conducted inspection trips and met with ICG executives, but none had made an offer, and Industries's management didn't seem to understand why.

Bruce knew, but couldn't seem to get Industries to understand—the ICG was just too big, its map too sprawling and riddled with money-losing branch lines to fit into another railroad's business plan. Bruce thought he had a better idea—break the ICG into pieces, sell off the parts that weren't working, and keep the parts that made sense.

Industries's management simply wouldn't tolerate any talk of piecemeal sales, and Bruce himself didn't have the numerical evidence that such a strategy would work. His intuition was telling him that the ICG should be broken up and sold off in pieces, but Bruce never acted on intuition alone. The other side of his temperament, plus his UT training, told him to get the facts first and document them numerically before making any bold moves. He needed to know what the ICG was worth as a whole—and in pieces.

The search for numbers begins

For help, he reached down to trusted and discreet subordinates from the Marketing Department, the late Doug Hagestad, now vice president of marketing, and Rick Bessette, a young number-cruncher who had started out as a junior analyst in the department and had been promoted by Bruce to director of market research.

Bessette understood the issue immediately and went to work producing what he called a Network Utilization Analysis. The NUA would document how the railroad actually was being used. It would ascertain which line segments were busy, which were not; which were making money and which were losing money, as well as which segments made sense for the ICG and which parts made more sense as part of another railroad. The NUA also would document what Industries did not seem to understand—that entrepreneurs could run a branch line profitably even when the ICG couldn't.

Within a couple of months, Bessette had documented what Bruce suspected. The original mission of the Illinois Central—to be a north-south railroad in an east-west world, hauling freight from Chicago and St. Louis to New Orleans, Mobile and Gulfport—was intact. The north-south main lines were doing a solid business and making money.

But the east-west branch lines the IC had accumulated over the decades, and especially the tangle of secondary lines and branches that came with the GM&O merger, were losing more money than the original main lines were making.

Basically, the branch lines were not covering their expenses because union agreements forced freight trains to carry a full crew—an engineer, a conductor and two brakemen to help the conductor pass hand signals to the engineer when switching cars. Walkie-talkies had made hand signaling obsolete, but the excess crewing persisted because the law made changing a union agreement almost impossible. Nobody seemed to know how to reduce those crew sizes.

New owners, new rules

Bruce knew how to do it—a federal judge had ruled that if a branch line were sold to a company that had never been in the railroad business, the new owner would not inherit the seller's labor agreements and could operate the trains with a smaller, non-union crew. The only catch was that the buyer could not be a railroad. It had to be a non-railroad company entering the railroad business for the first time. A start-up. Other railroads already had sold pieces of their map to startup entrepreneurs. Why not the ICG?

Bruce and Bessette package the product

Bruce had no strategy for persuading Bill Johnson to prune the ICG branch by branch. The official program at Industries remained—sell only the whole railroad—so Bruce and Bessette proceeded on a stealth basis, laying out a secret line-sales program to be disclosed only at such a time as Johnson gave the go-ahead.

First, Bessette identified each line segment that made commercial sense as an independent short-line railroad owned by a company that had never been in the railroad business and had no legacy union contracts. Then, he and Hagestad created a sales brochure for each segment. The brochure included each line's mileage, a map, a list of stations, photos of key infrastructure and buildings, junctions with other railroads, signaling technologies, grade crossings, bridges and viaducts, and the location and number of tracks in each yard. Each brochure listed the customers by name and the location of the sidings where the railroad accessed each shipper. The brochure showed the line's annual carloads and the commodities carried.

Each short-line package got its own code name, Newco 1, Newco 2, etc. A sale price was shown for each piece of line to be sold. The East Mississippi ICG had lines inherited from the GM&O, for example, which were packaged for quick sale at $22.5 million, or $31,000 per mile, a relatively cheap rate because the track was not in good condition. The Vicksburg Route, a busy and well maintained 403-mile bridge line from Meridian, Mississippi to Shreveport, Louisiana, was priced at $125 million, or $306,000 per mile, because it made sense as an extension of one of the big Eastern or Western carriers. Each brochure included a contact phone number at the ICG.

Bruce and Bessette now had a well-stocked store full of merchandise priced to move and priced to enrich the ICG. Their only problem was that they couldn't put it on the market. The official program at IC Industries was that the entire ICG would be sold in one piece.

"I don't know why Bill Johnson didn't understand our program," Bruce said. "He knew that those lines couldn't make money with trains operated by 4-man crews. And he had to know the law allowed start-up entrepreneurs to operate them with smaller crews; his own lobbyists had been active in writing the language of the Staggers Deregulation Act and they kept him informed about what deregulation would mean for the ICG.

"But I just couldn't convince him that selling off the piece parts made sense. He would only accept a sale of the whole railroad."

A fateful phone call changes everything

What solved Bruce's problem was a newspaper reporter facing a deadline without a good story.

Fragmentary rumors about Bruce's line-sales scheme had begun to trickle out, and some of the rumors had reached *Chicago Tribune* business reporter Sallie Gaines. As she sat at her desk in

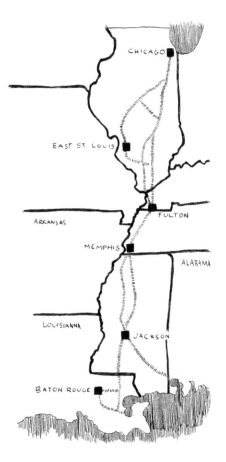

the twilight of a Friday afternoon in the fall of 1984, Gaines realized that she didn't have enough details for the edition due to hit the streets on Monday. Desperate, she called the ICG and asked to talk to Bruce.

"I understand you're looking to sell some lines, correct?" was Gaines's opening probe.

"Uh, we've been considering that, yes," replied Bruce.

"Well, which lines would you be interested in selling? I mean, if somebody offered to buy?"

"Well, what about the Iowa Line?" Bruce replied. "It's 777 miles long with branches and runs from Chicago to Omaha, Sioux City and Cedar Falls. It handles a lot of corn and soybeans out of Iowa and Northern Illinois."

Gaines pressed him further.

"O.K., what about the old Chicago & Alton?" he continued, warming to his subject. "285 miles from Chicago to St. Louis with a branch from Springfield to Kansas City. Lots of opportunities are there for an entrepreneur who knows how to identify new business opportunities."

His frustrated salesman instincts bubbling to the surface, Bruce began to gush about the enchanting possibilities of the GM&O branches serving the pulpwood plantations in East Mississippi and the potentially juicy export traffic at the end of the GM&O main line at Mobile. If buyers turned up with a serious business plan and financing for a purchase, he told Gaines, of course the ICG would talk with them.

On Monday morning Gaines's story ran, and a fuming Johnson called Bruce into his office.

"What do you mean, telling this woman we're entertaining offers to sell our lines?" Johnson stormed. "You know this isn't part of the plan. We're supposed to be keeping the whole railroad together so it can be sold to another Class 1."

While Bruce stood in Johnson's office having his ears fried in deep fat, Johnson's phone rang with a call from Bruce's secretary. Buyers were trying to reach him to start making deals for the branch lines. They were serious people, not amateurs or speculators. They had business plans, they had financing and they wanted to talk.

Let the sales begin

Bruce got back to his office and began returning phone calls. Johnson cooled down and, within a week, IC Industries had formally adopted Bruce's line-sales program. The first sale, the East Mississippi lines, was consummated eight months later for $22 million. With most of the Gulf, Mobile & Ohio trackage gone, Bruce eliminated the "Gulf" and changed the railroad's name back to Illinois Central.

Next went the line to Montgomery, Alabama, 42 miles that fetched $8.5 million. It was purchased, not by a startup company, but by a Class 1 railroad that needed to extend itself. On Christmas Eve, 1985, the Iowa Line was sold to an entrepreneurial group for $75 million, and, in the spring of 1986, the Vicksburg Route was sold to another well-bankrolled startup for $123.5 million. In the spring of 1986, the branch from Fulton, Kentucky to Louisville was sold to another startup, the Paducah & Louisville, for

$70 million, and in March 1987, the main line of the old Chicago & Alton from Chicago to St. Louis and the Springfield-Kansas City branch was sold for $81 million to an entrepreneurial startup called the Venango Corporation. In May, Bruce sold the money-losing 26-mile Illinois Central Electric commuter line from downtown Chicago to suburban University Park for $28 million. The buyer was Chicago's new publicly owned commuter-rail agency, Metra.

The final sale was particularly gratifying. One of the bright young stars of the IC's marketing department, Tom Hoback, raised $5.3 million and bought the 117-mile branch line connecting Indianapolis with the IC main line at Sullivan, Illinois.

Hoback went on to become a leader in the short-line industry, rapidly building up his line's traffic with coal, lumber, chemicals, grain, building materials, and even intermodal containers bringing Asian merchandise to the stores in Indianapolis. He poured the railroad's earnings into rebuilding track, bridges, and yards, making his little "branch line" into a mainline money maker and something of a model and showcase for modern railroad technology. The Indiana Rail Road was featured regularly in the railroad trade press and Hoback became a multi-millionaire as his short line surpassed anything it could have achieved had it stayed in IC ownership.

CHAPTER 14
SHRINKING THE PAYROLL

Getting rid of excess mileage was one problem. Getting rid of excess employees was another. Smaller though it was, the IC still had too many employees, and it had them everywhere—making up trains in the yards, manning trains on the main line, repairing trains in the shops, and shuffling paper in the offices. The IC always prided itself on being a "family" and it showed–relatives hired relatives, friends hired friends of friends, and they kept them around well after their utility had expired. People were hired without testing and assigned to tasks without any performance or aptitude evaluation.

Worst of all, most of the employees were union members working under agreements that made shedding them expensive. Under the Railway Labor Act, laying off an employee required a "Section 6" notice to the appropriate union, followed by continuing payments to the laid-off worker for a period based on the employee's seniority. Some employees could make almost as much money not working as they had while employed. Shrinking the employment roster didn't appear to make much sense if the payroll didn't shrink with it.

The answer was a job buyout, that is, identify the surplus employees and simply pay them to go away. Technically, a buyout is not a layoff because the employee decides whether to leave or stay. The union has nothing to say about it because a resignation is the employee's own decision, not something the company "does" to the employee.

How could Bruce persuade employees to accept a buyout when they liked their jobs? Unionized railroad jobs are lucrative, and employees rarely give them up in favor of other employment. Running a locomotive was one of the two or three best-paying jobs that didn't require a college education, and a conductor's job was not far behind. Why would those employees walk away from that kind of money?

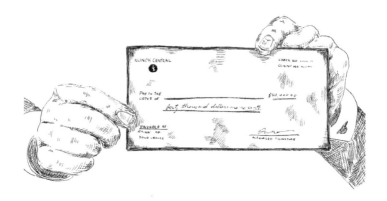

Show them the money

Bruce's solution was an original and highly persuasive scheme based on his experience at Murder Board-people act not just on information but on the way the information is presented to them. Instead of simply asking an employee whether he or she was interested in a job buyout, Bruce had a check for one year's wages made out in the name of each employee that a supervisor had deemed surplus.

The checks were turned over to the respective supervisors, and the supervisors were trained to follow a simple script-invite the employee into the office, show the employee the check and say "This check is yours today if you will agree to quit your job and leave the company. The taxes on the check already have been set aside by the company, so you get to keep the full face amount."

As Bruce had suspected, virtually all the targeted employees accepted the offer without hesitation. Faced with the largest check they had ever seen, usually as much as $40,000 to $50,000, the employee did a quick calculation and realized the check would pay off the mortgage, which usually was the family's largest expense. With their mortgage liquidated, the employee could take a lower-paying job in a convenience store, a fast-food outlet, or a doctor's office with no sacrifice in their family's quality of life. Some simply retired.

The banks willingly lent the new railroad the money for the buyout because the numbers were ironclad. Once the employee was gone, the railroad would recoup the employee's annual salary within a year and use the proceeds to repay the loan. All future savings were accrued to the railroad.

When the buyout program began in 1986, the ICG had 8,543 employees, but by the end of 1988, it had 3,164. The IC was a much smaller railroad now, slimmed down, profitable, much easier to operate and manage, and offering demonstrably higher value to its old customers and its growing list of new ones. Industries management had embraced and endorsed Bruce's vision of small is beautiful, and it showed.

And paid.

Tools of progress

Sometimes, it seemed as if the possibilities for economizing at the IC were endless. Bruce threw himself into the task, even counting tools. During a 1988 inspection trip at the railroad's giant locomotive and car maintenance facility, Woodcrest Shops, south of Chicago, Bruce was appalled at the primitive system the railroad used to keep track of tools, spare parts and solvents. All supplies coming into Woodcrest were ordered and recorded on paper, and everything requisitioned by the employees required another piece of paper, and, sometimes, it took days for a single piece of paper to migrate from the employee to the stockroom and another day or two for the required part or tool or chemical to be delivered to the employee who ordered it. At the company's giant Paducah Shops, the inventory management was even more primitive—a pair of ancient passenger coaches were being used as a tool crib. Any employee could walk in and walk out with a tool or spare part. There was no way to ascertain the pilferage rate.

The answer, of course, was computerization. Bruce detailed George LeCien from the computer department to digitize the entire inventory process, and LeCien developed one of the first barcoding systems used in the railroad industry. Every product used at Woodcrest and Paducah, from a barrel of track spikes to a diesel-locomotive cylinder to a roll of toilet paper, got its own barcode, and every station handling the item got a hand-held scanner to record its progress through the system. Pilferage dropped to zero, as did the waiting time for delivery. With instant information about the number of items remaining and the pace at which they were consumed, managers knew exactly when to reorder. The tool rooms never ran low on any item. The company saved about $15 million a year in purchasing and inventory costs.

CHAPTER 15

BUSINESS CAR
TO BUSINESS SCHOOL

In every job he'd held, Bruce had always found time to serve as a guest lecturer at the nearest college with a business school. As CEO of the IC, he adhered to that pattern, but with a difference–he no longer addressed classes at the nearest college or university. Instead, he delivered an evening lecture every Tuesday and Thursday at a school 127 miles south of IC headquarters in Chicago, the University of Illinois at Urbana-Champaign. Because Champaign is on the main line of the Illinois Central Railroad, Bruce traveled to his speaking engagements on the IC business car.

Harry Bruce was at the height of his career now, a plateau which he would continue to work on.

Time to tell the world

Although he has always been offended by braggarts and bullshitters, Bruce never hesitated to blow the horn when his team scored a victory. Good performance deserves applause, and he knew how to generate it. The IC's recovery merited that kind of attention, and Bruce was prepared to spend money on the best publicists and the latest technologies to make sure the world knew about it.

Even so, he never expected that his biggest publicist would be Mother Nature, or that she would work for free.

In the summer of 1987-88, the weather patterns in the Mountain West shifted, causing a radical reduction in the normal winter snowfall. By the spring of 1988, it had become apparent that the headwaters of the Missouri River would not be replenished at their normal rate. During what normally would be the period of the annual spring flood, the river was down two feet, then three, and then four. Barges and towboats no longer could operate on the Missouri.

The logistical disruption soon spread. The Missouri is a tributary of the Mississippi, and, by mid-summer, the Father of Waters was shrinking. Barge traffic on the Mississippi was halted. The riverfront docks where the barges loaded had dried up and become mud flats, unable to float even recreational watercraft. At Memphis, hardy locals were squishing across the Mississippi mud flats to inspect the exposed wrecks of riverboats that had lain undetected below the surface since the Civil War.

The situation was an economic disaster for farmers, country elevators, commodities traders, exporters, and food processors. When grain fails to move from the American heartland, factories close, employees are laid off, and global food prices skyrocket. The low-water emergency soon turned into a logistical nightmare. Midwestern riverfront elevators were bulging with millions of bushels of wheat, corn, barley, sunflower seeds, and soybeans waiting to be shipped to food processors or to oceangoing ships for export, but without barges the crops couldn't move.

"Our finest hour"

Into this crisis stepped the Illinois Central, in what Bruce, who never met a Churchillian expression he didn't like, calls "our finest hour." Most of the barge customers already were customers of the railroad. They relied on the IC to carry their grain locally from Iowa and Illinois elevators to the Mississippi for transshipment to barges.

Now that the rivers were dry, the IC marketing people started calling grain dealers to let them know the railroad stood ready to carry their grain all the way to destination, a thousand miles downstream to the giant elevators that stand along the Mississippi holding grain for shipment overseas in oceangoing bulk carriers. As the relieved shippers responded, IC went into the spot market and rented fleets of extra grain cars. Surplus locomotives were brought out of storage and quickly refurbished. Furloughed crew members were called back to work to run trains from Iowa and Illinois to the export elevators that stood between the IC tracks and the Mississippi at Reserve, Louisiana.

Never bashful about bragging, Bruce hired helicopters and film crews to shoot scenes of his grain trains bypassing barges stranded in the Mississippi mud and sent the tape to the TV networks. NBC Nightly News devoted several minutes of prime time to shots of multiple grain trains following each other out of the

IC's giant Markham Yard and onto the main line at Homewood, Illinois, then ran Bruce's hired tape with its overhead shots of IC grain trains passing grounded barges and towboats on the Memphis riverfront. The visuals made for good TV. Bruce put the IC squarely in the national spotlight, and print media soon followed.

Chicago Tribune reporter Bob Wiedrich was invited to ride the IC office car from Chicago to New Orleans behind a special train full of Illinois corn bound for overseas mills. Buoyed by the spectacle of a railroad's recovery, Wiedrich flew home and wrote a story lavishing praise on IC management and claiming he felt only one bump as the train covered the more than 900 miles between Chicago and New Orleans (with a 150-mile detour to the river-front grain terminals south of Baton Rouge).

Wiedrich's reference to the near-flawless track was meant to be congratulatory, but to those in the know it suggested an entire backstory. Had the IC not used that federal loan to rebuild the main line, and had the carrier not downsized, it would have remained too cumbersome and too poor to manage the huge ramp-up in traffic generated by the 1988 grain emergency. The controversial sell-off of branch and secondary lines and the pruning of the payroll by nearly half proved essential to creating a railroad rich enough, and poised and nimble enough, not merely to handle the emergency, but to profit from it and raise the company's profile.

Everybody knew about the IC now. What Alfred E. Perlman had done at the Rio Grande, the New York Central, and the Western Pacific, Harry Bruce had done at the Illinois Central, not just a corporate turnaround, but a transformation that made American business rethink its attitude about the entire railroad industry.

CHAPTER 16

INVESTORS NOTICE

Corporate stardom generally has a magical effect–the price of the company's stock rises as investors bid to become part of the success story and share in the growing profits.

That was not possible with the IC. It was still part of IC Industries, and investors could buy shares only in the conglomerate, not the railroad alone. The value the IC was adding to its parent remained impossible to estimate because IC Industries mingled the railroad's revenues with those of the bottling company, the industrial-refrigerator manufacturer, and the brake-shoe factory. Investors wanted to own the railroad, not the whole folder of companies in IC Industries' portfolio.

Industries Chairman Bill Johnson took the only possible course. At the end of 1988, he and the board voted to restructure IC Industries by establishing the railroad as a separate company to be spun off to the shareholders in shares they could trade on the New York Stock Exchange.

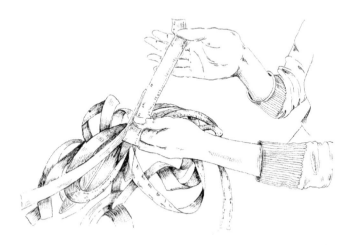

When the NYSE reopened after the New Year's holiday on January 3, 1989, bidding in the new IC shares was brisk.

One of the beneficiaries was Harry J. Bruce. When a successful subsidiary is spun off, the parent company typically rewards the corporate officers who made the company successful with large blocks of stock in the newly spun-off company. Harry Bruce was awarded 7.1 percent of the new company. For many years, Bruce had been successful, but he now stood to be rich.

During the late 1980s, the American corporate world had been rocked by a series of executive-compensation scandals. Bruce wanted none of that associated with the recovery and re-emergence of the Illinois Central.

A clean break

"I had no need to crown my success with a personal jet or a yacht," he recalls. "I wanted the shares distributed equitably and fairly to all the people who made the IC successful. I called a select group of senior staff together and asked them to devise a distribution schedule of shares to all management employees whose work contributed to the turnaround and to leave enough to award each rank-and-file employee with a minimum of ten shares."

To this day, Bruce is adamant that his act was not an expression of generosity.

"I was simply acknowledging that what we had done at the IC was done by a team," he said. "I may have been the leader, but you cannot talk about a leader without acknowledging that it is the essence of a leader's job to organize people into a team and direct a team effort to carry out the corporate plan and reach the goals set forth in the plan. Our team at the IC had done precisely that, and all the members deserved to be rewarded accordingly."

Market test

Bruce and his team had acted and they believed that they had done their job well. Now it was time for another actor, the market, to evaluate and reward their accomplishment.

Most observers who had watched the progress of the IC during its recovery speculated that, if the company were to be hived off by IC Industries, its shares would trade in the $10-$12 range. Although the company had made a spectacular turnaround from its dismal fortunes of the early 1980s, it remained relatively small for a Class 1 railroad, and, by shedding the GM&O along with its IC branch lines, it had reduced its annual revenues from $876 million in 1983 to around $500 million in 1988. The railroad was profitable, but it was smaller, and the experts believed only time would reveal its true worth.

On January 5, 1989, Bruce stood at the rostrum overlooking the trading floor of the New York Stock Exchange as IC shares were listed and trading began. Sales opened at the high end of the pundits' predictions: $11, a good sign.

On January 4 and 5, the price rose again. Traders and analysts seemed to agree that the new IC faced a future of reliable growth.

On January 15, one of the IC's largest customers, the Archer Daniels Midland Corporation, made an obligatory disclosure to the Securities & Exchange Commission that it had been accumulating IC stock for "investment purposes". ADM said its holdings amounted to 8 percent of the outstanding shares. A number in the 8-percent range usually means that the owner of the shares will demand a seat on the company's board of directors. Once ADM's disclosure hit the market, the share price rose to $15. On January 25, ADM announced that it now held 15 percent of IC shares, and the price per share shot to $22.

The share price sank slightly over the next couple of weeks, and rumors of further accumulations dwindled. Then, on February 20, a small New York investment firm, the Prospect Group, announced a tender offer which, if successful, would give it control of the IC Railroad. Prospect offered $20 per share for all outstanding shares.

"It's not ours to keep"
Bruce immediately called the board of directors together to examine their options. Some advocated searching for a white knight

to save the IC by outbidding the Prospect Group and leaving the current management in place. Others suggested a "poison pill" defense, such as amending the by-laws to make it impossible for a new owner to replace more than a third of the directors within the first year. Both strategies were popular during corporate-ownership struggles during the 1980s.

The IC's general counsel, Andrew Reardon, was in the boardroom during those debates and recalls how one of the directors suggested a third strategy that was popular during the 1980s, a management buyout.

"I can still remember it," Reardon said in a phone call from his Florida retirement home. "One of the managers said, 'Who can run the IC better than we can? We're the ones who created the new IC and made it successful. We know who the customers are and we know how the railroad works. We should be in control of the IC.'

"But Harry nixed it," Reardon recalled. "He said, 'No. We have no right to do that. It's not our railroad. It belongs to the stockholders, and only the stockholders have the right to pick the management.'

"I was very impressed with that," Reardon said. "It showed Harry was a true leader. He wasn't acting on behalf of himself. He was acting on behalf of others who had entrusted him with their property."

A "strict constructionist" on corporate governance
Bruce has since reiterated his position many times, sometimes to the media, but also to the business school students before whom he is frequently asked to appear.

"Many people have asked me since then why we didn't fight harder to keep the IC," Bruce said. "My answer is simple: the IC was not ours to keep. A corporation does not belong to its managers. It belongs to its stockholders, and under the law, they are entitled to the highest possible return on their investment."

Moreover, trying to hang on to their jobs at the IC would have made the railroad's managers look greedy, Bruce said. The stock that IC Industries had awarded them had doubled in value since they received it. Once Prospect bought them out, they would be rich, and none would be richer than Bruce.

Throughout his years as a business school lecturer, Bruce had been very out-front about the poorly understood concept known as corporate governance – the corporation is owned by its shareholders and the shareholders elect a board of directors to oversee management to make sure it acts on the shareholders' behalf. Now, as the Illinois Central came into play, it was more essential than ever to make clear that the interests of the shareholders would prevail in the boardroom.

"I am a strict-constructionist on corporate governance," Bruce says, and his conduct in those early days of 1989 proved it.

Knowing when the party's over

On March 17, 1989, the Prospect Group completed its accumulation of IC shares and took the company private. Bruce took the transition as his signal to retire. Like so many of his personal decisions, this one was based on the same mix of intuition and calculation that had guided him safely through career inflection points in the past. He had seen too many successful executives linger "too long at the fair" and experience told him that he was now approaching some sort of invisible watershed beyond which the victories would become increasingly elusive.

Nor was his decision based entirely on intuition.

"I had followed the careers of many successful CEOs, and for most of them the 'arc of success'—the period when they were really hitting their stride—usually lasted no more than six or eight years," he said. "A lucky few kept the fun going for ten years. I had been at the ICG and IC for 14 years, the last six as CEO. Continuing in that capacity would have been 'pushing it.'"

Finally, there was Vivienne.

"She was very sick with an irreversible deterioration of the spinal nerves that had left her paralyzed," Bruce said. "The doctors were unable to arrest her condition, and we had round-the-clock nurses attending her at home. I belonged at home too."

Bruce had arrived at that stage of life when giving back becomes important. With a grant of $1 million, he endowed the Harry and Vivienne Bruce Chair in Transportation Economics in the University of Tennessee School of Business.

Vivienne Jennings Bruce died in March, 1996. She was survived by her husband, three children, and a grandchild.

.

CHAPTER 17

FLORIDA ON HIS MIND

Bruce may have retired from corporate management, but he never retired from his parallel career of writing and teaching, and retirement gave him plenty of time for both. His contact with the University of Tennessee School of Business intensified, and he became particularly close to the Dean, Warren Neel, who suggested Bruce's next teaching job. Since 1980, Bruce had owned a condo in Fort Pierce, Florida and Vivienne had been spending more and more of her time there as her condition worsened.

"When I told Dean Neal I had settled in Florida and I wanted to start teaching again he said, 'I know the business school dean at Florida Atlantic University.' Florida Atlantic at that time was still small, not the powerhouse it is today. The business school was glad to have a retired corporate executive, and I was glad to be lecturing again."

As Florida became his new permanent home, Bruce sold the Fort Pierce condo and bought a larger home in North Palm Beach. Bruce continued his lecturing and indulged in golfing, always his preferred form of recreation.

A second priority had been gestating in his mind for several years, and now it had grown to the point where it demanded his full attention.

The pen is mightier...

That project was writing. Throughout his career Bruce had always published articles on transportation, supply-chain management, and economic geography in small professional journals. Now, he wanted to break out into a wider arena and publish works of more general interest on topics in demand with business students, regardless of specialty.

His first try, "A Short Guide to Business Writing," was published in an anthology compiled by UT English professors Russel K.

Hirst and Michael L. Keene in 1995. Ever since his exposure at
U.S. Steel to that amateurish and ineffective report on automated
movement of materials, Bruce had been increasingly critical of
the typical American business report, and with his training as a
public speaker, he knew that most executive speeches were duds.
He now set forth his remedies–shorter, punchier sentences and
paragraphs. Less biz-school jargon and careless borrowing from
pop culture. Instead, he proposed paying closer attention to the
sounds of words and expressions, which are absorbed by listeners
differently from the way they are absorbed by readers.

He also shared his public-speaking expertise, warning against
trick words like "nuclear"–he said Americans' keep scrambling
it into "noo-kyuh-ler" –and cautioning after-dinner speakers to
skip the free meal in order to keep their minds and mouths sharp
to maintain a clear delivery of the speech and prompt response
to listener questions during the Q & A. ("You can always go out
and enjoy some nice broiled grouper after your speech is over," he
wrote).

Finally, Bruce introduced American business students to a new
type of document designed specifically to enhance a young manager's career prospects–the Portfolio of Accomplishments.

"The typical professional resume is lacking in firepower because
it lists only the different positions the applicant has held," Bruce
wrote. "It doesn't necessarily say what the applicant did in those
positions, and it usually is silent on the dollar value the applicant
contributed to each employer in each position held."

The Portfolio of Accomplishments fills those gaps.

"It sets forth not just the names of the positions the applicant held but the dollarized value the employee created for the employer while serving in each position," Bruce said.

"For example, my own Portfolio of Accomplishments states explicitly that, during my tenure at U.S. Steel, my initiative in creating a heated tank car for carrying pitch enabled my employer to book $30 million worth of new business per year. When a prospective employer sees an applicant's past performance set down in numbers like that the effect is phenomenal-no guessing. The job applicant is a known quantity and a hiring decision can be made quickly."

Inside the world of American corporations

Bruce's concerns were not limited strictly to the way American business managers wrote and spoke. Reviewing his own career, and particularly his work in turning the Illinois Central Gulf around, he felt an increasing degree of alarm over how they were thinking and acting. The three decades in which Bruce had risen from corporate recruit to chief executive officer had been years of turmoil in American business as one fad after another—conglomerization (which was only to be followed by spinoffs), management by objectives, management buy-outs, leveraged buyouts, hostile takeovers, and dizzyingly costly bankruptcies—roiled the once placid surface of big business. What was going on?

Bruce had no grand scheme to explain it all, but he did have his suspicions, and one of them was that too many American business managers, up to and including CEOs and corporate boards, had forgotten the legal and moral principles under which publicly traded businesses were organized, the laws of corporate governance.

What people don't know about the board-management relationship

Bruce summarized his views in a groundbreaking 5,000-word cover story titled "Duty, Honor, Company" that appeared in the Winter 1997 issue of *Directors & Boards* magazine. Too many corporate managers and directors, Bruce reminded his readers, had simply forgotten that a corporation is organized under the law as a fiduciary for its shareholders.

Fiduciary, from the Latin *fides*, faith, means that the managers of the corporation are legally obliged to be faithful to the shareholders, who provide the corporation with its funding but, under the law, are not considered owners but holders of equity in the company, and thus must entrust the management of the company to professionals. Those professional managers are legally obliged to act in the interest of the shareholders by growing the value of their investment, and the directors making up the board are morally and legally obliged to make sure that management is doing its job and must replace the chief executive officer if the company fails in that obligation.

Bruce summarized the fiduciary duty of a corporate director in three simple components:

- *Directors are there to hold the CEO and his or her associates accountable for preserving and enhancing shareholder value.*
- *The chief tool they use to exercise this accountability is their power to hire, evaluate, and replace the chief executive officer.*
- *Existing law gives them all the power they need to carry out these functions. Tinkering with the rules is not needed. Obedience to the rules is.*

Poorly managed corporations did not need any new legal penalties to prevent disaster, Bruce wrote. The boards of directors already had all the legal authority and the obligation to replace the management. The problem was, not enough of them were doing so. The Penn-Central bankruptcy, the harrowing collapse of Enron, Sunbeam, and dozens of smaller corporations suggested that corporate boards were not doing their job and that many corporate directors didn't even understand what their job was.

The editors of *Directors & Boards* thought Bruce's essay so essential—and so clearly reasoned and documented—that they devoted the front cover to a color photo of Bruce posed in front of an Illinois Central locomotive heading up a piggyback train loaded with new semi-trailers. Silver-haired and clad in a three-piece blue suit with a gold watch chain across the vest, Bruce looked every inch a railroader and a CEO, but the text of his story made clear he knew a lot more than how to make the trains run on time. He had thrown a glass of ice water in the face of American business management.

CHAPTER 18

WHAT IS LEADERSHIP?

Bruce got plenty of responses to his remarks on business writing, and his efforts to refocus corporate boards on the full depth of their legal obligations were welcomed, although sometimes warily, by the other corporate directors in his circle.

One subject continued to preoccupy him–leadership. The shelves in American bookstores were groaning under a swelling collection of titles purporting to explain and teach leadership, and business school libraries held even more, along with master's theses and doctoral dissertations purporting to examine, if not always explain, what qualities made certain people into those that other people followed.

Bruce plowed through a sampling of the most popular titles but emerged vaguely dissatisfied. Different authors identified different leadership traits, but many of the same traits could be found in other individuals who were not leaders. There was widespread disagreement as to what made certain people leaders and what made other people follow them.

Bruce's curiosity about leadership took a fresh turn in 2000 when one of the meetings of Dean Neel's Advisory Council brought him into contact with UT Professor of Marketing Ernest Cadotte, who, with his wife, had established an educational software company, Innovative Learning Solutions. Ernie was working on a new marketing textbook, *The Management of Strategy in the Marketplace*.

Ernie's plan for the book was to have eleven separate chapters on different aspects of marketing, each contributed by a different author, including one by himself. After talking with Bruce, he agreed that the book needed two additional chapters not specifically related to marketing–an expanded treatment of Bruce's *Directors & Boards* cover story on corporate governance and a closing chapter focused on leadership.

The Management of Strategy appeared in 2008 and has been in print ever since. Despite its intimidating size, it remains a favorite with students of marketing because of its huge trove of practical, tested principles and the depth, knowledge, and experience of its contributors.

The most popular chapters in the book are not about marketing at all. Bruce's chapters on corporate governance, and especially his chapter on corporate leadership, remain perennial favorites with the students. Student reaction to Bruce's leadership chapter was so strong that Dr. Cadotte published it as a separate book, *Lessons in Leadership*.

The leadership puzzle

In the book's first chapter, Bruce took an original approach to
the matter of leadership. After examining several dozen books
and articles on the subject, Bruce began to review the careers of
corporate leaders that he himself had met or had worked for, as
well as the case histories of several other highly successful business leaders that had come to his attention. His survey disclosed
something earlier authors had missed, a type of behavior Bruce
called "leadership without portfolio."

"Each of the successful business leaders I studied first emerged as
a leader by successfully undertaking a task that their superiors
had never asked them to perform, and for which in many cases
they were not trained or even prepared," Bruce said. "In some
cases they even lacked the authority to solve the problem, probably because their superiors were not even aware that a problem
existed and hence never thought about who might be qualified to
solve it."

Bruce couldn't help observing that his decision to re-evaluate and then jump-start U.S. Steel's abandoned interest in computerized transport had an element of leadership without portfolio in it.

"Gayton Germane suggested we look into why the project was abandoned, but the decision to pick up the dropped threads and resume the search for a solution was mine," he said. "None of my superiors ordered me to do it."

When he began sharing the idea of leadership without portfolio with some of his fellow CEOs, Bruce hit paydirt. He was pleasantly surprised to find that each of them also had an episode of leadership without portfolio, usually never examined or remarked upon, early in their careers.

"We don't need a training program"
One example was Ray Tower, who rose to become CEO of FMC Corporation (formerly Food Machinery & Chemical Corp). In 1955, when he was 30 years old, Tower was an eastern district sales manager for one of the company's chemical divisions, a post with little power or authority but lots of restrictive rules and traditions. Soon after he was hired, Tower realized his unit had no formal training program for the new salesmen it was hiring, and when he suggested one to his superiors they not only rebuffed it but suggested he not pursue it any further.

The snub didn't stop Tower. Despite the rigidity of FMC's classic mid-'50s organizational structure and his superiors' explicit rejection of his idea, Tower forged ahead on his own, developing a salesman-training program and putting it into effect. He even told his bosses what he had done and let them know his training program had improved the sales staff's performance. He said his disclosure was "met with total apathy" until, one day, word came down that Corporate wanted to review the training programs of all the company's divisions.

Top management had become sold on training programs and wanted to evaluate all such company-wide programs that were in effect. Tower's boss, panicky over his department's lack of a program, demanded a copy of the plan Tower had been using on his own trainees and passed it off to Corporate as a policy of the entire department. The feedback from Corporate was positive. Later, the same superior who had rejected Tower's plan sheepishly apologized for his earlier dismissal of the initiative and told Tower that Corporate deemed his plan one of the best in the company.

There is no quicker route to advancement than making your superiors look good, and Tower's rise now became rapid. In addition to exercising leadership without portfolio, Tower had also displayed another quality common in leaders.

"He was persistent," Bruce said. "The initial rebuffs he received did not discourage him. Instead of advocating harder for his proposal, he simply proceeded to put it into effect and let the results make his case for him."

As Bruce reviewed the case histories submitted to him by friends and colleagues who had reached the CEO level, he found similar examples, and Leadership without Portfolio kept turning up like a bad penny.

"It's like hearing a new word and looking up the definition," he said. "Once you learn the word you start hearing and seeing it everywhere."

Leadership without portfolio launches Lee Iacocca's career

Lee Iacocca's best-selling 1984 autobiography provided another key. It never mentioned the term "Leadership without Portfolio", but Bruce identified it as key to Iacocca's spectacular career rise in 1956 when he was a lowly assistant sales manager at Ford's floundering Philadelphia district, the worst-performing in Ford's national sales network. Desperate to start moving cars, Iacocca offered to have his dealers finance Ford sales for 20 per cent down and $56 per month for three years—a figure he thought "almost anyone could afford." He named the innovation "$56 for '56." Within three months, the Philadelphia district's sales shot from last in the nation to first.

Ford CEO Robert McNamara said Iacocca's innovation was responsible for selling an extra 75,000 cars. Iacocca was reassigned to Ford headquarters in Dearborn, first as national manager of truck sales, and then as the architect of the program that launched the biggest automotive success of the late 20th century, the Mustang.

Why does Bruce call Iacocca's initiative Leadership without Portfolio?

"Because he had no authority to do it," Bruce said. "I checked with a CEO friend of mine who was working at Ford at the time, and he said dealer financing of car sales was unknown in 1956. Anyone who wanted to purchase a car on time got the financing from a bank, and any discounting of vehicle prices had to originate in Detroit. Lee Iacocca didn't just pioneer, he stepped way out of line. He dared. We can only speculate what would have happened to him if his initiative had failed."

Bruce said Leadership without Portfolio is not solely the property of chief executive officers. It can be found at any level of an organization and can drive outstanding performance regardless of rank.

Master of the railroad tracks

His favorite example is the late Bill Knight, who Bruce met when Knight was superintendent of engineering for the Illinois Central Gulf's trackage between Memphis and New Orleans.

"Despite the name 'engineering' in his title, Bill had never been to engineering school," Bruce wrote in Lessons in Leadership. "He undoubtedly would have made an excellent engineer if he had had the opportunity, but Bill was from rural Mississippi, where few families had the money to send a child to college in 1945, the year 16-year-old Bill joined the railroad."

As a substitute for a college education, Knight worked his way up from a lowly track laborer to executive by mastering every task and every fact needed to build and maintain the railroad's physical infrastructure.

"His knowledge of his job was encyclopedic," Bruce said. "He worked incessantly and asked questions wherever he went, absorbing details until he seemed to know every classification yard, every length of rail, every tie in the hundreds of miles of line entrusted to his care. What Bill Knight exemplified in his style of leadership was a core competency so vast that it amounted to virtual mastery of the subject. Subordinates and superiors alike were awed by his knowledge and came to depend upon it."

There was another dimension to Bill Knight's leadership that transcended his mastery of facts, figures, and dimensions.

"Everyone could tell that Bill cared deeply about the safety and effectiveness of the railroad plant," Bruce said. "It was not just his knowledge and his competence but his values that made people follow him."

Did Bill Knight launch his career with an episode of leadership without portfolio?

"I was not around when Bill embarked on his employment with the railroad, so I have no way of knowing whether leadership without portfolio played a role in the early phase of his development as a leader," Bruce said. "But he definitely had that quality of daring, initiative and willingness to take on risk by the time I met him."

The proof came one night during the critical period when the ICG was downsizing in the mid-1980s. Although IC Industries had accepted Bruce's scheme to sell some of its surplus trackage, not all of the surplus mileage was likely to find a buyer. The company owned three different routes between Memphis and Jackson. All of them were losing money and one of them had to be eliminated without delay. The law said that if a railroad abandoned a stretch of track and another railroad wanted to operate it, the new operator could use the track without paying for it.

Bruce casually mentioned to Knight, "You know, we need to get out there and pull that track up one of these days before somebody else decides to use it." Without seeking written permission or setting a date, Knight immediately organized a work train and crew and dismantled the line, reclaiming the used rail and ties for use elsewhere on the railroad. He acted so quickly that part of the operation took place during the middle of the night during a violent thunderstorm as patrons at a rural cafe next to the tracks watched the work going forward during flashes of lightning. Some of the alarmed patrons called the Mississippi Highway Patrol to investigate the scene, and the governor of Mississippi even called Bruce for an explanation, which was accepted.

"Bill was simply exercising leadership without portfolio," Bruce said. "He didn't seek formal approval for what he did. He understood that the need for action was urgent and he knew he and his crews were capable of delivering the necessary outcome, so he took the initiative himself and did what was necessary."

Leaders transcend themselves
Bruce says Bill Knight's values provided him with the missing piece he needed to complete the puzzle of leadership.

"The textbooks spend a lot of time analyzing the personal traits and properties of leaders, but that's not where the secret of leadership ultimately lies," he said. "You can't construct a leader out of a set of traits the way you construct a building out of lumber, bricks and steel. Real leadership has something transpersonal about it, something that keeps the followers focused on something beyond the leader to a set of values."

Bruce says this realization dawned on him as he observed and responded to the behavior of his hero, Alfred E. Perlman.

Why leadership succeeds even when it's not nice

"In many ways Perlman confounds the usual prescription for leadership," he said. "He had great vision, encyclopedic knowledge, an amazing capacity for identifying and cultivating talent and a sovereign ability to establish strong, clear goals.

"At the same time he could be petty, fussy and downright nasty in his treatment of his subordinates. His temper tantrums were legendary, especially when he criticized underperformance. Yet his managers esteemed him, admired him and, when he criticized them they followed his counsel and worked to improve their performance. Very few quit, and most self-corrected and incorporated Perlman's standards into their own work."

What were those transpersonal values that inspired Perlman and enabled him to build high-performing teams that turned three sick railroads around?

"I think Perlman's insistence on excellence was more than a personal thing with him," Bruce wrote in his 2003 memoirs, *Mentors and Memories*. "What really drove it was his feeling for the railroad industry, which he desperately longed to restore to its former position of respect and admiration. The low esteem in which the railroad industry was held by outsiders hurt him. He seemed to feel a personal responsibility to win that esteem back and redeem the industry in the eyes of its critics. His mission was to prove that railroads—certainly any railroad that he ran—could provide just as much service to customers and just as much return on investment to the shareholders as any of the businesses that enjoyed higher levels of respect."

Bruce said he found it "particularly suggestive" that all three of the railroad turnarounds spearheaded by Perlman came before deregulation.

"Alfred Perlman was as persistent and articulate in denouncing regulation as anyone in the industry," Bruce said. "But unlike many other railroad executives at the time he refused to blame regulation as an excuse for underperformance. Instead of waiting for deregulation to 'free' the railroads to improve, he just forged ahead and led all three of the railroads where he worked to superior performance. He wanted deregulation, but he refused to sit and wait for it, and he was very short-tempered with railroaders who used regulation to rationalize their own underperformance. In fact, he hated excuses of any kind. A subordinate who pleaded an excuse immediately provoked his wrath."

Because his employees sensed his devotion to a principle beyond himself, they acknowledged Perlman as a leader and followed him, Bruce said. That leadership became the gift that kept on giving. Perlman's managers absorbed his lessons in leadership, developed leadership styles of their own, and went on to success at other railroads as well as non-railroad businesses.

"They trusted his vision even when they themselves could not see what he beheld," Bruce said. "We all knew that he saw it, and that was good enough for us."

Bruce said his own leadership style is "not a clone of Perlman's."

"My own values were oriented more toward the shareholders," he said. "Having studied corporate governance, I understood management's obligation to the people who put up the money, and when the Illinois Central was spun off and publicly traded, I insisted the board act on their behalf. That was not a set of values that all CEOs pursued in the late 1990s, but it was mine, and I have never regretted that decision."

Bruce said his Army training may have helped him develop a leadership ethic.

"To be a successful Army officer, you have to acknowledge the idea of being in service to others and in service to an ideal," he said. "Your other talents and ambitions may carry you far, but without that sense of obligation to some kind of higher value, those gifts alone will not make you a leader. Leaders have big egos. That means they need a big set of transpersonal values to make sure their leadership gifts work in a positive way."

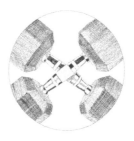

EPILOGUE

HERE AND NOW: KEEPING BRUCE—AND THE RAILROAD INDUSTRY—FIT

As of this writing, Harry Bruce is 92 years old and lives in retirement in North Palm Beach, Florida. Four days a week, he goes to the Odyssey Athletic Club in Palm Beach for a complete workout–stretching exercises, weight lifting, core development, and aerobic routines under trained instructors. He's in great shape and, except for a pacemaker installed in 2005, has no health problems. He says he's been doing cardio-fitness exercises for at least 40 years, moving to a new gym or fitness center whenever his career took him to a new job.

After Bruce retired from the IC, it continued to prosper under Prospect Group's management. As predicted, deregulation proved a boon to the railroad industry, and, as the 1990s unfolded, the profits of all the carriers soared, degraded track was restored to the highest levels in history, and technological, managerial, and marketing innovations won back old customers and began attracting new ones. The railroad industry still lagged motor carriers in revenues and profits, but market share began to increase, expenses continued to drop and profitability increased. A new generation of Americans grew up without seeing the term "railroad bankruptcy" in the headlines.

In 2009, the nation's most admired investor, Warren Buffett, bought the 23,000-mile Burlington Northern Santa Fe Railway for $47 billion, calling his purchase "an all-in bet on the future of the American economy." Alfred E. Perlman would have been proud. Respectability had been restored to the industry he loved.

"Precision?" Really?

One of the major players in this dramatic new phase of the industry's evolution was a swaggering Tennessean named E. Hunter Harrison (1944-2017) who joined the post-Bruce Illinois Central in 1989 as vice president and chief operating officer and was elevated to chief executive officer in 1993. When the IC was purchased by the giant Canadian National Railway in 1998, the CN board promoted Harrison to CEO of the entire CN system.

Harrison, a silver-haired, booming-voiced executive who favored Mafia-style pin-striped suits, immediately shook up the transportation world with a new train-operating scheme he called Precision Scheduled Railroading. Under PSR, he said, every loaded freight car was to have a "trip plan" which showed when it would be picked up from a shipper's siding, which trains would carry it, and the times and locations for where it would be sorted in the classification yard before on-time delivery to a receiver's siding.

The North American railroad world watched as CN's revenues and profits soared. As helmed by Harrison, Precision Scheduled Railroading seemed to be the elixir that would take the industry to the next level in its astounding recovery. When Harrison moved from Canadian National to head its rival Canadian Pacific in 2011, he installed PSR at that railroad, and when he came back to the U.S. and became head of CSX Corp., he made PSR that carrier's operating system too. Soon, CSX's rival, Norfolk Southern, announced that it too would operate its trains on the PSR model, and shortly thereafter Union Pacific fell into line with a PSR program of its own. Only Buffett's BNSF stood on the sidelines.

Bruce remained one of the skeptics.

"Precision Scheduled Railroading does not by itself account for the success of Canadian National under Hunter Harrison's administration," he said.

"The Canadian economy was booming because the world was recovering from the financial panic of late 1998. New housing starts created a huge demand for lumber from British Columbia, and as the job market recovered so did driving and demand for crude oil from Alberta and Saskatchewan. Food production increased, meaning the Canadian railroads were moving more hopper cars of wheat, barley, sunflower and canola seeds, along with lots of potash to make fertilizer for American farmers. In retrospect, it's very hard to attribute any growth in railroad profits to PSR."

By 2021 Bruce's skepticism began to look justified. On the U.S. side of the border, PSR seemed to have been vulgarized from its original goal of crisp scheduling into simply a way to squeeze more profit out of every train movement. Typical freight-train length doubled from one mile to two—so that a single crew was effectively handling two trains instead of one—but the giant trains were so long they didn't fit into the sidings. Meeting and passing trains on single track became a cumbersome process that lengthened each trip and ruined the schedules promised to shippers.

By the spring of 2022, major shipper groups were complaining to their congressmen about the deterioration in freight service, and the House Transportation Committee was holding a hearing on the problem—switch crews were failing to position cars on schedule for loading and car shortages were making it impossible for shippers to keep their commitments to customers. The Surface Transportation Board began calling railroad CEOs to Washington to explain the problem and the possible solutions.

Bruce watched from his retreat in Florida and smiled.

"Precision Scheduled Railroading was oversold from the beginning," he said. "It was not the reason for Canadian National's success under Hunter Harrison, and by the time it reached the U.S., it was just another ploy to goose productivity by running longer trains with fewer crews."

Having some fun with the failure

Nevertheless, Bruce found something compelling in the term "Precision Scheduled Railroading," and in the winter of 2020, he found it. The COVID 19 pandemic was causing a rapid loss of membership at his favorite workout site, the Odyssey Athletic Club. Public-health authorities had warned Americans that heavy breathing inside a closed space was an ideal way to spread germs, and across the nation the health-conscious gym patrons complied. The Odyssey lost members, and soon it was losing money, including funds it had set aside for building maintenance.

Bruce never dropped his membership. He lent the Odyssey funds to tide it over the crisis. It survived, made the necessary repairs, and repaid the loan.

Bruce also supplied the Odyssey with the outlines of a marketing program, including some impromptu advertising copy: "Come visit the Odyssey Athletic Club, where shaping your future is not accomplished by dumbbells," he wrote.

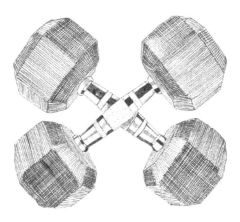

"Your Odyssey trainer will plan a program that meets your personal design, shape and configuration needs.
"Come on in and see—your first visit is free!"

Then Bruce concluded his Odyssey marketing program with a tongue-in-cheek mission statement.

The Odyssey Mission:
Precision Scheduled Training, engineered and conducted to keep your physical vitality on track.